MONTAIGNE IN CAMBRIDGE

MONTAIGNE IN CAMBRIDGE

PROCEEDINGS OF THE
CAMBRIDGE MONTAIGNE COLLOQUIUM
7-9 APRIL 1988

edited by

Philip Ford and Gillian Jondorf

CAMBRIDGE FRENCH COLLOQUIA
CAMBRIDGE · 1989

Contents

In memoriam
O. M. H. L. de M.

Acknowledgements

We should like to thank Dorothy Coleman and Liz Guild for their help in the organisation of the Colloquium. We are extremely grateful to the following institutions, whose generosity made both the Colloquium and the publication of these proceedings possible: the British Academy; the French Cultural Delegation in Cambridge; the French Embassy, London; Clare College, Cambridge; Downing College, Cambridge; Gonville and Caius College, Cambridge; New Hall, Cambridge; Robinson College, Cambridge; Trinity Hall, Cambridge. Our thanks also go to the Master of Clare College, Professor R. C. O. Matthews and Mrs Matthews for permission to use the Master's Lodge for the Reception, and to Dr Peter Hutchinson for showing us the sixteenth-century library of Trinity Hall.

Introduction

Following the success of the 1985 Ronsard Colloquium, the organisers decided to follow it up three years later with a second colloquium to commemorate the 1588 edition of Montaigne's *Essais*. Once again, the Colloquium took place in Clare College, where scholars from France and Britain were invited to give papers in three main areas: Montaigne's use of quotations; his use of language; and the changing text of the *Essais*. Once again, also, both the papers and the ensuing discussion proved to be extremely fruitful, with a relaxed atmosphere encouraging contributions from Montaigne specialists and non-specialists alike.

Since Montaigne, unlike Ronsard, did not set foot in the British Isles, we cannot nurture the thought that he may have passed through Cambridge; Montaigne was, nevertheless, very much present in our thoughts during the papers. It was the French visitors, Michel Magnien and Daniel Ménager, who concentrated on Montaigne's use of quotations. In a wide-ranging paper, Michel Magnien approached the paradox in Montaigne that, while despising all forms of imitation, he fills his writings with quotations from the ancients — not, however, in the traditional way, where such allusions are a primary aid to *inventio*, but rather to adorn his style in a process he refers to as 'application'. However, once present, these quotations may recall their original contexts to produce a dialogue not only with Montaigne's own text but also between themselves. Daniel Ménager takes a particular example of quotation, Montaigne's allusions to Lucretius, the second most quoted poet in the *Essais* after Horace. Viewed in the Renaissance as 'philosophus et poeta', Lucretius is examined in this paper to see which of the two roles was uppermost in Montaigne's own conception of him. As an 'interlocuteur privilégié' rather than a mouthpiece, Lucretius is most appreciated by Montaigne when his philosophy is least dogmatic, but beyond that, his poetry contains something special which means he cannot simply be paraphrased like other philosophers, and which leads Montaigne to quote him even when he disapproves of the sentiments he is expressing.

It is on the language of Montaigne that the British contributors chose to concentrate. Though he was unable to be present, M. A. Screech has provided a characteristically scholarly paper on the dangers of reading Montaigne without the necessary classical and biblical background, illustrated with examples in four main areas. John O'Brien considers the question of paradox in the chapter 'De la phisionomie': if, as was generally agreed, a beautiful soul is reflected in a beautiful face and body, how is it that Socrates was proverbially ugly? This question leads the author to consider the use of paradox as a rhetorical device and the whole relationship between words and things. James Supple also chose to concentrate on a single chapter in book III, 'Du repentir', to examine what precisely Montaigne means by repentance, a question which introduces the whole problem of Montaigne's religious beliefs. Finally in this section, Keith Cameron investigates word-play in the *Essais*: is it there to be thought-provoking and to suggest subtle readings of the text, or is Montaigne just amusing himself and being gratuitously witty?

Dorothy Coleman produced the only contribution on textual considerations in the *Essais*, showing how the autograph corrections of the *exemplaire de Bordeaux* can add to our understanding of Montaigne, not least because they show the author reading himself as if he were another person.

One session of the Colloquium is not represented by any formal account in the following pages. This was an informal discussion, introduced by Dudley Wilson, of 'De l'oisiveté' (I. 8. 32-3), chosen for its brevity which enabled the chapter to be considered as a whole. Thus it formed a contrast to the Colloquium papers which either traced a theme or problem across a number of chapters, or looked at certain aspects of one long chapter. One point on which discussion focused was the circularity of the imagery used in 'De l'oisiveté', returning at the end of the chapter to the images of procreation and of horsemanship used in the opening sentences. The quotations (all in verse, one each from Virgil, Horace, Martial, and Lucan) also attracted attention, and it was remarked that the two already present in the 1580 text (Horace: 'velut ægri somnia, vanæ / Finguntur species' and Lucan: 'variam semper dant otia mentem') are closely in line with the main theme of the chapter; Lucan uses the very word ('otia') from which the title of the chapter comes, and Horace's terms are also close to words such as 'imaginations', 'folie', and 'rêverie' used by Montaigne. The Martial quotation added in 1588 ('Quisquis ubique habitat, Maxime, nusquam habitat') seems to be supplying the original of what Montaigne had already quoted in translation in the 1580 edition ('c'est n'estre en aucun lieu, que d'estre par tout'). The Virgil quotation, however, with its beautiful image of a flickering light-spot, reflected from the surface of a pot of water on to a wall or ceiling, introduces both a completely new image and a more attractive view of the imaginings produced in idleness, previously likened to 'herbes sauvages et inutiles' and 'amas et pieces de chair informes'. Given that the whole chapter has a strongly prefatory or programmatic air, the ambivalence introduced by the Virgil quotation could perhaps be seen as representative of tensions and ambivalences in the work as a whole.

If 'De l'oisiveté' could be seen as prefatory (although not used as preface by Montaigne), so too could Odette de Mourgues's paper be read as prefatory to the Cambridge Montaigne Colloquium. There is, however, another reason for placing it at the head of this volume. Odette was a devoted admirer of Montaigne, but had never published anything on him, so the organisers of the Colloquium (all of whom had been taught by her) were jubilant when they persuaded her to contribute a paper. In its perceptiveness, delicacy, and wit it is vintage Odette. It is also her last publication. Only a few weeks after the Colloquium, Odette de Mourgues contracted pneumonia, and died on 1 July 1988. With great admiration, and great affection, we dedicate this volume to her memory.

Editors' Note

Unless otherwise stated, all references to Montaigne are to *Les Essais de Montaigne*, edited by Pierre Villey, with a preface by V.-L. Saulnier, 2 volumes (Paris, 1978), and are given in the form of book number in Roman figures, chapter number in Arabic figures, and page number in Arabic figures, with the 1580, 1588, and 1595 editions indicated, where appropriate, by a, b, and c.

The following abbreviations have been used in the notes:

BHR	*Bibliothèque d'Humanisme et Renaissance*
BSAM	*Bulletin de la Société des Amis de Montaigne*
CAIEF	*Cahiers de l'Association International des Etudes Françaises*
MLR	*Modern Language Review*
THR	Travaux d'Humanisme et Renaissance
TLF	Textes Littéraires Français

Passé, présent, futur dans les *Essais*

Odette de Mourgues

Le titre de ma communication peut sembler ambigu. En fait il ne s'agira pas de grammaire ou presque pas. Les quelques remarques que je vais faire sur le voyage à travers le temps, et même parfois hors du temps, dans lequel nous entraîne la lecture des *Essais* n'est qu'une sorte d'introduction par la bande à certains des thèmes au programme de ce colloque.

Le passé, c'est évidemment pour Montaigne l'Antiquité, cette culture grecque et latine qu'il a absorbée par ses lectures. Non seulement il proclame sa dette envers Plutarque et Sénèque, mais il ressort des nombreuses citations dans son ouvrage que s'est créée une intimité profonde entre lui et les écrivains, poètes ou prosateurs, qu'il cite, ne serait-ce que dans le fait qu'il lui arrive de modifier le texte cité. C'est là le genre de liberté qu'on ne saurait prendre qu'avec des amis. Question fascinante que je laisse à d'autres participants le soin d'éclaircir.

Il y a un autre aspect du rôle que joue dans les *Essais* cette vaste et riche culture gréco-latine. Pour celui qui lit Montaigne pour la première fois, les citations d'Horace ou de Lucrèce, les anecdotes de Plutarque ou de Pline, les considérations étendues sur la vertu de Socrate, font sur lui un peu le même effet que les soi-disant digressions de Balzac sur le tempérament allemand ou les erreurs de la municipalité parisienne. Le lecteur s'apercevra bientôt que ce monde antique se révèle comme étant dans les *Essais* quelque chose d'assez spécial et une dimension importante dans l'architecture de l'œuvre. Il n'est pas question de vérité historique. Montaigne n'en a cure. Ce qui l'intéresse, c'est quelque chose de bien plus général, comme il l'explique au chapitre 21 du livre I, c'est de retrouver 'un tour de l'humaine capacité' (I. 21. 105c). Il n'est pas responsable des jugements que porte Tacite ni de la véracité d'Hérodote, et peut en liberté faire tous les commentaires qu'il lui plaît. Les Grecs et les Romains qui peuplent les *Essais*, que ce soient des écrivains comme Sénèque et Virgile, des héros de l'Antiquité comme César et Caton, ne sont pas à proprement parler des personnages historiques. Ils font partie d'un univers imaginaire qui, bien qu'imaginaire, est très solide d'abord parce qu'il repose sur une tradition reconnue et honorée, et ensuite parce que cet univers est constamment soumis à ce qu'on pourrait appeler la critique psychologique de Montaigne basée sur son expérience du réel.

Il a d'ailleurs et par deux fois (livre II, chapitres 10 et 31) exprimé la curiosité qu'il a 'de connoistre l'ame et les naïfs jugemens de mes autheurs' (II. 10. 414-15a). Ainsi non seulement les écrivains mais aussi Alexandre, Socrate, Epaminondas, toute une foule de guerriers, d'hommes d'état, de philosophes, de matrones romaines émergent du monde de la littérature et de l'histoire et deviennent autant d'acteurs dans une sorte de vision intemporelle de la nature humaine qui est celle de Montaigne, et qui peut être la nôtre. Ils ne sont plus figés dans le passé avec une épitaphe définitive. Ils prennent une personnalité plus vivante, plus ambiguë aussi car si d'un côté ils appartiennent à une époque révolue, d'un autre côté Montaigne nous donne à penser qu'ils n'ont pas encore dit leur dernier mot, que l'on peut encore exiger qu'ils répondent à certaines questions, qu'ils expliquent les motifs de leur conduite, les raisons de certaines attitudes qu'ils adoptèrent. Voyons Caton par exemple. Dans le chapitre 37 du premier livre il a déjà pris ses distances à l'égard du jour fatal où il se tua dans Utique et il apparaît comme une image épurée et aggrandie de ce qu'il fut et cela à travers un siècle de littérature latine d'Horace à Martial dans les vers de cinq poètes que cite Montaigne. Il pénètre ainsi dans l'univers montaignien, enchâssé dans une précieuse substance poétique, par le truchement d'un plaisir esthétique. Ailleurs il est plus directement présent. Dans le chapitre 11 du livre II les sentiments qu'il dut éprouver lors de son fameux suicide intriguent Montaigne. N'y avait-il en lui que l'impassibilité du stoïque? S'approchant de son héros avec précaution, par une série de mouvements ponctués par des 'ce me semble', 'je croy', 'sans doute', il découvre et fait revivre ce qui dut être chez Caton l'intense jouissance de l'acte gratuit ou mieux, pour citer Montaigne, 'la beauté de la chose mesme en soy' (II. 11. 425a). Socrate aussi s'est admirablement conduit avant sa

2

mort, mieux peut-être même, pense Montaigne, qui ajoute 'Caton me pardonnera, s'il luy plaist; sa mort est plus tragique et plus tendue, mais cette-cy [celle de Socrate] est encore, je ne sçay comment, plus belle' (*ibidem*). Je trouve ce 'Caton me pardonnera' extrêmement touchant et significatif: ce futur dans le présent; car c'est ainsi qu'on s'excuse à l'avance auprès d'un ami qui d'un moment à l'autre va vous faire part de ses réactions.

Socrate bien entendu est le personnage le plus important chez Montaigne dans tout son ouvrage et jusqu'à la fin. Vous vous rappelez sans doute comment dans les dernières pages des *Essais* il lui reproche gentiment ce qui est à ses yeux son seul côté faible: 'ses ecstases et ses demoneries' (III. 13. 1115c). Peut-être le plus beau rôle que lui confie Montaigne dans le chapitre 12 du livre III est d'être son porte-parole. Socrate 'courageux en la mort, non parce que son ame est immortele, mais par ce qu'il est mortel' (III. 12. 1059c) surgit du passé révolu et dans un long passage modelé à partir d'emprunts faits à Platon, prononce de nouveau son plaidoyer devant ses juges et exprime ainsi les propres idées de Montaigne sur ce que doit être une attitude raisonnable devant la mort.

Tels sont le genre d'échanges à travers les siècles que nous trouvons dans les *Essais*. Montaigne se met à la place de Caton, Socrate à la place de Montaigne. Pour nous aussi, lecteurs un peu désorientés par les facettes miroitantes des spéculations de Montaigne, ces hommes d'Antiquité sortent de l'histoire, deviennent des êtres familiers, un peu troublants parfois, comme si au tournant d'un paragraphe l'un d'eux venait derrière nous pour nous taper doucement sur l'épaule.

Mais ce téléscopage du passé, du présent, et du futur nous affecte aussi d'une autre façon.

J'aborderai le second point de mon exposé par quelques remarques sur l'*Apologie de Raimond Sebond*, ce long chapitre qui a donné lieu à tant d'interprétations touchant la religion de Montaigne. Celle qui semble le mieux concilier les contradictions apparentes que contient le texte nous propose de voir en Montaigne un fidéiste — le fidéisme, comme vous le savez, consistant en une séparation radicale entre la sphère de la foi et celle de la raison. Dorothy Coleman dans son ouvrage nous met très justement en garde contre ce genre d'étiquette apposée sur Montaigne,[1] et de fait le fidéisme représente des attitudes très différentes les unes des

3

autres. Tout dépend de la façon dont s'opère la séparation entre les deux sphères. Il est intéressant de voir ce qu'il en est chez Montaigne et de préciser le scepticisme qui provoque la coupure. La raison pour laquelle Montaigne considère la raison humaine incapable d'atteindre aucune vérité, de saisir aucune réalité, est qu'au départ, suivant la philosophie de son temps, il conçoit vérité et réalité en termes d'essence et d'absolu. C'est à cause de cette impossibilité d'arriver à l'essence des choses que Montaigne méthodiquement et de façon très impressionnante détruit la valeur du langage, de nos sens, de tout, et en vient à la conclusion: 'Nous n'avons aucune communication à l'estre' (II. 12. 601a), 'estre' signifiant 'essence'. Sur ce point, l' *Apologie* pourrait être considérée comme une des meilleures expressions de la faillite de l'essentialisme. Une conception essentialiste de l'univers conduit à une impasse totale: le langage est infirme, les activités intellectuelles de l'homme telles que les sciences sont dénuées de sens, la liberté est un leurre puisqu'il est impossible de prendre une décision valable. Que choisir quand le critère appartient au monde des essences que nous ne pouvons pas connaître? La défaite de l'essentialisme prend de telles proportions dans l'*Apologie* qu'on serait tenté d'y voir la preuve par l'absurde de la valeur de l'existentialisme. En fait ce que Montaigne semble faire c'est de confier ce monde inconnaissable des essences à la religion. Après quoi il peut approcher la réalité sous un autre angle là où il peut la saisir jusqu'à un certain point: en lui-même. Ceci donne un aspect particulier au fidéisme de Montaigne. On ne saurait mettre en doute la sincérité de son catholicisme, mais je dirais que dans son cas la sphère de la foi apparaît comme n'étant rien de plus que le magnifique sarcophage de l'essentialisme défunt.

J'ai mentionné l'existensialisme: un anachronisme de ma part mais assez caractéristique de certaines réactions d'un lecteur du vingtième siècle. Réactions assez excusables car la pensée de Montaigne transcende souvent la période de la Renaissance. Il y a en particulier dans les *Essais* ce que j'appellerai des échos prospectifs, échos de ce que de futurs penseurs ou écrivains découvriront par eux-mêmes. Entendons-nous bien. Il n'est pas question ici de l'influence de Montaigne. Je ne vais pas parler des plagiats de Pascal, ni du pastiche de La Bruyère, ni des mille emprunts ou allusions faits à Montaigne. Il s'agit ici d'une forme très spéciale d'intertextualité, et même, je dirais, d'une forme

4

aberrante puisque le lien entre un passage des *Essais* et le texte futur n'existe que dans la pensée du lecteur. Ainsi je lis dans l'*Apologie* la remarque de Montaigne: 'Et certes la philosophie n'est qu'une poësie sophistiquée' (II. 12. 537c), et je pense à toutes ces pages dans les *Cahiers* de Paul Valéry exprimant la même chose. On a dit qu'il était difficile de ne pas songer à Proust de temps en temps en lisant les *Essais*. Vous vous rappelez la fameuse critique que Proust adresse à la littérature réaliste qui cherche à décrire la réalité objective: 'Seule la perception grossière et erronée place tout dans l'objet, quant tout est dans l'esprit.' Il y a dans le chapitre 50 du premier livre un très beau passage dans lequel Montaigne montre combien est pauvre et douteuse la vision de choses autour de nous comparée à la connaissance subjective de ces mêmes choses:

> Les choses à part elles ont peut estre leurs poids et mesures et conditions; mais au dedans, en nous, elle [âme] les leur taille comme elle l'entend....La santé, la conscience, l'authorité, la science, la richesse, la beauté et leurs contraires se despouillent à l'entrée, et reçoivent de l'ame nouvelle vesture, et de la teinture qu'il lui plaist: brune, verte, claire, obscure, aigre, douce, profonde, superficielle, et qu'il plaist à chacune d'elles: car elles n'ont pas verifié en commun leur stiles, regles et formes: chacune est Royne en son estat.
>
> (I. 50. 302c)

La première phrase du passage nous rappelle le caractère incertain, et en tous cas inconnaissable, de ce que pourrait être l'essence des choses; et ce monde des idées est de fait traduit par une liste de termes abstraites: santé, conscience, etc. A ces concepts objectifs Montaigne oppose toutes les qualifications concrètes — brune, verte, etc. qui transforment ces abstractions dès qu'elles sont en nous en autant d'expériences individuelles, originales, dont la réalité vivante est exprimée en termes de couleurs variées, de jeux d'ombre et de lumière, de sensations diverses. C'est là la seule réalité perceptible, et Montaigne en souligne l'absolue royauté: 'chacune est Royne en son estat.'

Même la grande découverte de Proust, la valeur de la mémoire involontaire, se trouve dans les *Essais*. Montaigne découvre que ce ne sont pas les efforts volontaires qui déclenchent les mouvements de son esprit: comme il le note dans le chapitre 10 du premier livre, l'impulsion est donnée par des 'occasions estrangeres, presentes et fortuites' (I. 10. 40a). Les trois adjectifs sont significatifs: 'estrangeres' — qui n'ont rien à voir avec ce dont il s'agit; 'fortuites' — un simple coup du hasard; 'presentes' — ce n'est pas un souvenir abstrait qui met en branle le mécanisme de la pensée mais quelque chose qui appartient à la réalité vivante autour de lui. En somme toutes les conditions qui seront remplies lorsque Proust goûtera la madeleine trempée dans la tasse de thé.

Ainsi nous rencontrons dans les *Essais* des hommes qui ne naîtront que des siècles plus tard. Un commentaire de Montaigne (I. 25. 144c) sur de glorieuses victoires dues à des raisonnements fautifs, à l'imprévoyance, ou même simplement à l'inaction vient tout à coup vous rappeler des considérations sur la stratégie militaire dans *La Guerre et la paix* de Tolstoï.

Que de rencontres inopinées pour le lecteur de Montaigne. Dans le chapitre sur la diversion (III. 4), Montaigne constate que la plupart du temps les réactions de notre sensibilité ne sont provoquées que par des images superficielles, par les 'vaines escorces' d'un sujet (III. 4. 836b). Nous sommes émus par le son des mots, par le ton de la voix. Ce qui nous afflige c'est le gémissement de compassion qui n'est qu'une 'plainte grammairiene et voyelle' (III. 4. 837b), et il suffit de l'attouchement d'une main amie pour éveiller la crainte de la mort. Nous avons là, subtilement amorcée, la théorie du philosophe William James sur les émotions: à savoir que ce n'est pas l'émotion ressentie qui dicte notre comportement mais l'inverse. Nous ne tremblons pas parce que nous avons peur mais nous avons peur parce que nous tremblons.

Ces quelques exemples que je viens de donner semblent être, de la part de Montaigne, autant de gloses, sur Valéry, Proust, ou les philosophes du dix-neuvième siècle. 'Nous ne faisons que nous entregloser' (III. 13. 1069b), a-t-il dit, mais quelle grande originalité chez lui que d'avoir ainsi glosé sur des textes qui n'existaient pas encore.

NOTE

1 *Montaigne's Essays* (London, 1987), p. 171.

2

'Latiniser en Françoys': citation et imitation dans les *Essais*

Michel Magnien

'Qui suit un autre, il ne suit rien' (I. 26. 151c). Peut-on remettre l'imitation en cause avec plus de violence qu'avec cette boutade tardivement insérée dans l'essai 'De l'institution des enfans'? A son habitude, Montaigne consacre ici une rupture par rapport aux habitudes intellectuelles contemporaines. Depuis l'Antiquité, l'imitation avait été — pour la morale comme pour le style — le fondement même de tout apprentissage: le jeune esprit se devait de tenter à toutes forces de ressembler aux *paradeigmata*, aux *exempla* à lui proposés ou par lui élus, de les suivre sur leurs illustres traces.

Avec Montaigne, nous entrons dans l'ère du soupçon: l'imitation n'a plus de réelle efficience: les animaux produisent des effets 'ausquelles il s'en faut tant que nous puissions arriver par imitation que, par imagination mesme, nous ne les pouvons concevoir' (II. 12. 468a). A côté de Socrate et de Caton, Montaigne se contente d'évoquer 'leurs imitateurs (car de semblables, je fay grand doubte qu'il y en ait eu)' (II. 11. 425c).

On l'aura compris, Montaigne ne croit plus aux vertus de l'imitation. Et il emploie presque toujours ce terme (et ceux de sa famille) dans une intention de dénigrement; sur les quarante-six occurrences des *Essais*, seules un peu plus d'une douzaine appartiennent à un contexte positif; et encore les *exempla* proposés aux lecteurs sont-ils dans trois cas les animaux (II. 12. 465b, 481a, 490a) ou la 'sotte simplicité' des 'gens de la commune' (III. 12. 1049b). Modèles bien paradoxaux.

En matière politique, à l'heure des guerres civiles, l'imitation est éminemment pernicieuse: 'si les inventeurs sont plus dommageables,

les imitateurs sont plus vicieux, de se jetter en des exemples, desquels ils ont senty et puny l'horreur et le mal' (I. 23. 119c). L'époque corrompt les 'natures debonnaires': 'La longue souffrance engendre la coustume, la coustume le consentement et l'imitation. Nous avions assez d'ames mal nées sans gaster les bonnes et genereuses' (III. 12. 1042b).

Si telle est la sévérité du philosophe et du gentilhomme, face à l'imitation, quelle sera l'attitude de l'écrivain? Nous verrons dans un premier temps comment Montaigne démontre l'impossibilité de l'imitation, puis comment ce refus de l'imitation le conduit à la citation. Dans un troisième moment, nous analyserons les conséquences de ces choix sur la forme, voire sur le fond de son œuvre.

* * *

En matière de style, le constat est tout aussi pessimiste: tout ce que l'imitateur saura retenir de son modèle — Erasme l'avait déjà affirmé[1] — sera ses défauts:

> Or j'ay une condition singeresse et imitatrice:...Ce que je considere, je l'usurpe: une sotte contenance...une forme de parler ridicule. Les vices, plus:...On m'a veu plusouvent jurer par similitude que par complexion.
>
> (III. 5. 875b)

L'imitateur se tient toujours à la surface, se montre incapable de rendre le *pectus*,[2] de reproduire les qualités de l'auteur favori:

> L'imitation du parler, par sa facilité, suit incontinent tout un peuple; l'imitation du juger, de l'inventer ne va pas si vite. La plus part des lecteurs, pour avoir trouvé une pareille robbe, pensent tresfaucement tenir un pareil corps.
>
> La force et les nerfs ne s'empruntent point; les atours et le manteau s'emprunte.
>
> (I. 26. 172c)

Où l'on retrouve Erasme, qui dans le *Ciceronianus* avait raillé les vains efforts des Cicéroniens pour imiter le Père de l'éloquence, alors qu'ils n'en possédaient pas toutes les qualités. L'imitation est une 'baye' (I. 26. 169a), car chaque individu est unique, possède un *genius* qu'il est impossible de forcer. Comment le disciple pourra-t-il, dans ces conditions, reproduire le maître? 'La dissimilitude s'ingere d'elle mesme en nos ouvrages; nul art peut arriver à la similitude' (III. 13. 1065b). 'On peut naître Cicéron, on ne saurait le devenir', avait déjà affirmé Erasme.[3]

L'imitation sera toujours stérile car — nous l'avons vu — elle ne peut reproduire qu'une forme; et l'on sait, entre les *res* et les *verba*, où va la préférence de Montaigne. Les émules de Ronsard et de Du Bellay demeurent ainsi 'court à imiter les riches descriptions de l'un et les delicates inventions de l'autre' (I. 26. 171a). L'imitation ne peut conduire qu'au psittacisme; et rôde dans les pages des *Essais* le bestiaire constitué dès l'Antiquité pour flétrir les mauvais imitateurs, les singes (III. 5. 875-6c) ou le perroquet (I. 25. 137a).

Loin de suivre Quintilien lorsqu'il assurait que 'artis pars magna contineatur imitatione',[4] Montaigne va jusqu'à remettre en cause l'utilité et l'idée même de modèle, lui qui s'instruit 'mieux par contrarieté que par exemple, et par fuite que par suite' (III. 8. 922b), et qui n'hésite pas à lancer: 'une mauvaise façon de langage reforme mieux la mienne que ne faict la bonne' (*ibidem*).

Face à un grand homme, face à un grand texte, ce n'est plus une volonté d'émulation, mais un sentiment d'admiration qui envahit Montaigne, alors aussi interdit que devant les 'coups de main' de la Providence, 'qu'il nous faut, non pas imiter, mais admirer...qu'il est folie et impieté d'essayer à représenter, et que nous ne devons pas suivre, mais contempler avec estonnement' (I. 23. 121c). Attitude devant le divin, attitude devant la 'divine poesie' des anciens, le parallèle est tentant:

> Quand j'escris, je me passe bien de la compaignie et souvenance des livres...à la verité, les bons autheurs m'abattent par trop et rompent le courage.
>
> (III. 5. 874b)

> ...les productions de ces riches et grandes ames du temps passé sont bien loing au delà de l'extreme estendue de mon imagination et

souhaict. Leurs escris ne me satisfont pas seulement et me remplissent; mais ils m'estonnent et transissent d'admiration. Je juge leur beauté...si avant qu'il m'est impossible d'y aspirer.

(II. 17. 637a)

Impiété, impossibilité, Montaigne n'a ni le cœur ni, à l'en croire, les moyens d'imiter. Il rompt en ces pages avec toute une tradition rhétorique: la perfection engendre l'admiration et non plus le désir de rivaliser,[5] aucune volonté de *certare cum* — comme le manifestent si souvent les imitateurs d'alors.[6] 'Je ne luitte point en gros ces vieux champions là, et corps à corps...Je ne m'y ahurte pas' (I. 26. 147-8c). On est fort loin du credo cicéronien, de la fougue d'un Scaliger ou d'un Dolet que la difficulté aiguillonnait et poussait au travail; loin aussi en définitive des aspirations des poètes de la Pléiade pour qui les anciens demeuraient des modèles à égaler, voire à surpasser 'en nostre langue'.[7] Comme naguère Erasme, Montaigne préfère *mirari* à *imitari*, *sequi* à *adsequi*:

encore que les coupures & cadences de Saluste reuiennent plus a mon humeur, si est ce que ie treuve Cæsar & plus admirable & moins aysé a imiter.

(II. 17; texte de 1580, II. 438)

C'est qu'à ses yeux, le style doit être le reflet, voire le témoin des qualités de celui qui écrit, non de ses lectures; à travers le discours, *pictura sive speculum animi*,[8] chaque *genius* doit pouvoir se révéler. Mais les pédants et leur éloquence d'école ont tout bouleversé:

Nous sommes chacun plus riche que nous ne pensons; mais on nous dresse à l'emprunt et à la queste: on nous duict à nous servir plus de l'autruy que du nostre.

(III. 12. 1038b)

En un siècle où la compilation, la paraphrase, le plagiat règnent en maîtres — jusqu'en maintes pages des *Essais* — leur auteur montre une bien curieuse obsession de l'authenticité:[9]

quand nous voyons quelque belle invention en un poëte nouveau,

10

quelque fort argument en un prescheur, nous n'osons pourtant les en louer que nous n'ayons prins instruction de quelque sçavant si cette piece leur est propre ou si elle est estrangere; jusques lors je me tiens tousjours sur mes gardes.

(III. 8. 940b)

Chez 'un homme sçavant', 'il faut sçavoir ce qui est sien et ce qui ne l'est point' (*ibidem*). Montaigne semble donc bien refuser, en matière de style, la théorie de l'innutrition développée à travers la métaphore alimentaire par l'Antiquité et reprise à son compte par Du Bellay[10] et la Pléiade. Notons que la fameuse image des abeilles pillotant 'deçà delà les fleurs' (I. 26.152a), empruntée à Horace ou à Sénèque,[11] n'est plus ici appliquée au style mais — glissement significatif — au jugement de l'enfant. Parallèlement, Montaigne ne cesse de souligner la crudité de son 'parler' (I. 40. 253b); il produit des 'effects de nature crus et simples' (III. 2. 805b). Au sujet de ses 'imaginations', il affirmait déjà en 1580:

Elles sont naturelles et toutes miennes. Je les produisis crues et simples, d'une production hardie et forte, mais un peu trouble et imparfaicte; depuis je les ay establies et fortifiées par l'authorité d'autruy, et par les sains discours des anciens, ausquels je me suis rencontré conforme en jugement.

(II. 17. 658a)

* * *

Ici encore se produit une véritable révolution rhétorique; le processus habituel — tel qu'on le voit décrit par exemple chez Quintilien — qui via la lecture, la traduction, la paraphrase, ou l'imitation conduit à la composition, est totalement inversé: Montaigne, et il le répète en six passages au moins,[12] écrit *avant* de lire; et paradoxalement, plus il écrit, plus il lit: a préexisté une 'forme', qu'il a fallu par la suite emplir de 'matière'.[13] La triade classique *inventio-elocutio-dispositio* n'a plus lieu d'être; elle est confondue en une nouvelle notion, empruntée elle aussi métaphoriquement à la nature: la 'conception',[14] cette fécondité naturelle du *genius* qui engendre d'elle-même l'idée structurante et le mot juste.

11

> Je n'ay aucunement estudié pour faire un livre; mais j'ay aucunement
> estudié pour ce que je l'avoy faict, si c'est aucunement estudier que
> effleurer et pincer par la teste ou par les pieds tantost un autheur,
> tantost un autre; nullement pour former mes opinions; ouy pour les
> assister pieç'a formées, seconder et servir.
>
> (II. 18. 666c)

On ne saurait plus clairement marquer son refus de toute imitation, de
toute innutrition stylistique, voire morale. Souvenons-nous de la comparaison des oiseaux qui 'portent [le grein] au bec sans le taster, pour en
faire bechée à leurs petits', et de 'nos pedantes [qui] vont pillotant la
science dans les livres, et ne la logent qu'au bout de leurs lévres, pour la
dégorger seulement et mettre au vent' (I. 25. 136a). Sous la plume d'un
gentilhomme qui craint plus que tout d'être confondu avec 'un de ces
latineurs de college' (I. 26. 168a), ce qui pourrait passer pour une
description de sa propre pratique de la citation est pour le moins
troublant. Mais là encore, Montaigne ne dénonce une pratique que pour
mieux démontrer la singularité de la sienne; car il est sûr que les
innombrables citations dont il parsème ses *Essais*, plus que des preuves
d'une absence de digestion, sont les indices d'un refus d'assimilation.

S'il peut se permettre de citer, et de citer plus que sans doute tout
autre auteur contemporain, sans passer pour un cuistre, c'est justement
qu'il a rompu avec le procédé classique de l'imitation, qu'il qualifie de
'meurtriere' (III. 5. 875c):

> ...quand je me meslois de faire des vers (et n'en fis jamais que des
> Latins), ils accusoient evidemment le poete que je venois derniere-
> ment de lire; et, de mes premiers essays, aucuns puent un peu à
> l'estranger.
>
> (III. 5. 875b)

La citation, désormais seconde, n'informe plus l'*inventio*, mais participe
de l'*ornatus*:

> ...ces parements empruntez...je n'entends pas qu'ils me couvrent, et
> qu'ils me cachent: c'est le rebours de mon dessein, qui ne veux faire
> montre que du mien, et de ce qui est mien par nature.
>
> (III. 12. 1055b)

12

Mais pourquoi alors cette omniprésence explicite du texte tiers — la présence implicite pouvant être masquée par la mauvaise foi? Montaigne en donne la raison aussitôt après le passage que nous venons de transcrire:

> [B] et si je m'en fusse creu, à tout hazard, j'eusse parlé tout fin seul. [C] Je m'en charge de plus fort tous les jours outre ma proposition et ma forme premiere, sur la fantasie du siecle et enhortemens d'autruy.
>
> (III. 12. 1055)

Les citations seraient donc une concession au goût du jour. Etrange assertion de l'auteur, au moment même où il affiche sa volonté de révéler sa nature profonde, affranchie de toute influence extérieure; et puis, comme l'ont déjà prouvé bien des études,[15] sa pratique de la citation est trop systématique, informe trop son texte, pour ne constituer qu'un 'amas de fleurs estrangeres' (III. 12. 1055b).

Si l'on songe au processus d'appropriation des sentences à l'œuvre dans les *Essais*, on peut en partie résoudre ce paradoxe. Peu sensible à l'argument d''authorité', plein de dédain pour l'étalage d'une 'suffisance relative et mendiée' (I. 25. 138b), Montaigne livre rarement le nom de l'auteur qu'il cite (ou alors s'il le nomme, il le traduit en le citant: I. 14. 58a, I. 53. 310a, I. 55. 314a, II. 14. 611a); il déforme également les fragments cités de deux manières: en en modifiant parfois la lettre, plus souvent en les arrachant à leur contexte, et en leur conférant par l'insertion dans son propre discours un tout autre sens. Une méthode assez développée pour qu'il ait jugé utile de lui donner un nom au chapitre 26 du premier livre: c'est 'l'application' (I. 26. 147c). Le terme sera repris et commenté dans son contexte originel par Mlle de Gournay en 1635; et paradoxe, pour la fille d'alliance, l'application devient une des formes de l'invention:

> Les emprunts sont si dextrement adaptez, que le benefice de l'application, ou maintefois quelque enrichissement dont il les rehausse de son cru, contrepesent ordinairement le benefice de l'invention...Et me semble qu'il ait encores quelque chose de nouveau et de peculier, en delices et floridité perpetuelles, comme aussi l'a-til en l'excellence et delicatesse dont il applique...ses emprunts...en sorte qu'autant d'applications, ce sont presque autant de belles inventions.[16]

13

Il est sûr que Montaigne 'tord à luy les sentences' (I. 26. 171c), qu'il leur 'pein[t] le crin et la queuë,...les esborgne' (III.12.1056, n. 19), qu'il ose leur 'changer d'assiete et de jour' et les 'enfoncer' (III. 8. 937b).[17] Considérons la première citation des *Essais*, au chapitre 2 du livre I:[18]

> Voyla pourquoy les poëtes feignent cette misérable mere Niobé...avoir esté en fin transmuée en rochier,
> *Diriguisse malis.*
>
> (I. 2. 12a)

Au parfait ovidien, Montaigne a substitué l'infinitif passé afin d'insérer le latin dans la trame syntaxique française. Mais surtout, contrairement à ce que l'introduction de la citation pourrait faire croire, il n'a pas retenu le vers des *Métamorphoses* qui contenait le mot *saxum* (VI. 309), il est remonté plus haut, au début du passage, afin de choisir les deux termes les plus suggestifs, les plus 'bastants' (III. 9. 994c), ou les plus 'vehements' (I. 26. 171c), pour reprendre sa terminologie.

Cette méthode fait irrésistiblement songer à celle des auteurs de *motti* qui, comme vient de le montrer C. Balavoine,[19] extraient de leur texte déjà composé une formule significative, la plus expressive, sinon la plus transparente, afin de 'réduire, condenser, discrètement obscurcir' le sens général de leur pièce. Ici, Montaigne a forgé d'après Ovide un véritable *motto* qui résume et illustre d'une manière parfaite les exemples de tristesse qu'il vient d'évoquer, Psammenitus, Charles de Guise, Agamemnon, et enfin Niobé. Et Montaigne nous paraît jouer sur les deux sens du mot — l'antique et le moderne — lorsqu'il qualifie ses citations d''embleme[s] supernumeraire[s]' (III. 9. 964c): comme des images, elles sont insérées dans le texte qu'elles ornent, et comme elles, elles entretiennent avec le contexte, qu'elles doivent à la fois illustrer et prolonger, des rapports complexes.

* * *

Montaigne l'affirme d'ailleurs lui-même: on ne saurait voir dans les citations de simples motifs décoratifs:

> mes allegations ne servent pas toujours simplement d'exemple,

14

d'authorité ou d'ornement...Elles portent souvent, hors de mon propos, la semence d'une matiere plus riche et plus hardie, et sonnent à gauche un ton plus délicat, et pour moy qui n'en veux exprimer d'avantage, et pour ceux qui rencontreront mon air.

(I. 40. 251c)

Pour être véritablement comprise, la citation exige du lecteur 'une veuë oblique' (III. 9. 994b); elle se trouve par là même bel et bien intégrée au processus d'écriture. Elle devient l'une des composantes du style nonchalant, de cette 'alleure poetique, à sauts et à gambades' (III. 9. 994b) élus par Montaigne pour rompre en visière avec l'éloquence cicéronienne;[20] la citation participe de cette esthétique du surgissement, du 'mot serré' (III. 9. 994c), qui 'signifie plus' qu'il ne dit (III. 5. 873c). Le lien du fragment étranger (dont l'altérité est soulignée — comme dans tout ouvrage contemporain — par l'italique) avec son contexte ne va pas toujours de soi; mais lorsque le diligent lecteur l'aura saisi, c'est tout le passage qui acquerra un sens et une portée supplémentaire: 'Je ne dis les autres, sinon pour d'autant plus me dire' (I. 26. 148c).

Mais pourquoi dire les autres, s'il 'se veut faire voir jusques au dedans' (II. 17. 647a)? C'est qu'ils disent parfois mieux que lui. En effet, dans l'ordre qu'il s'est donné, le *sermo brevis*, le latin se montre supérieur:

je fay dire aux autres ce que je ne puis si bien dire, tantost par foiblesse de mon langage, tantost par foiblesse de mon sens.

(II. 10. 408c)

à me reconnoistre, au prix de ces gens là, si foible et si chetif, si poisant et si endormy, je me fay pitié ou desdain à moy mesmes.

(I. 26. 146a)

Par crainte du pédantisme, le gentilhomme de la Chambre du Roi a en effet décidé de 'corrompre [sa] plume' (I. 40. 250c), d'adopter un parler 'qui tire...un peu vers le dedaigneux' (I. 40. 253b);[21] mais surtout, il a choisi de s'exprimer 'en vulgaire' (au risque qu'on croie 'la conception et le dessein, vulgaire de mesmes' (II. 10. 408c)). Cela n'allait pas de soi, étant donné que 'le langage latin [lui] est comme naturel' (III. 2. 810b); d'autant plus que cette manifestation suprême de *sprezzatura* mène à une aporie, souvent dénoncée par Montaigne lui-même: cet 'idiome' est 'plus foible' (II. 12. 440c), moins "ferme' (III. 9. 982b) que le latin; il 'fléchit', il 'succombe...à une puissante conception', et alors le latin 'se présente au secours' (III. 5. 874b). En fait, Montaigne s'est interdit d'user de l'instrument capable de traduire au mieux ses aspirations stylistiques, d'aboutir à ce 'parler simple et naif...succulent et nerveux, court et serré' (I. 26. 171a) qu'il goûte plus que tout. Et l'on sent comme un regret à cet abandon forcé: 'le latin me pippe à sa faveur par sa dignité, au delà de ce qui luy appartient' (II. 17. 634c).

Puisque le latin est proscrit, puisque l'imitation est contraire à sa conception de l'être et de l'écriture, ne reste qu'une solution pour démontrer le prestige de la langue latine: l'emprunt. Mais un emprunt de 'naturaliste' (III. 12. 1056c): l'idée est sienne; le vêtement seul appartient à autrui, et se montre comme tel:

> Je m'en vay, escorniflant par cy par là des livres les sentences qui me plaisent, non pour les garder, car je n'ay point de gardoires, mais pour les transporter en cettuy-cy, où, à vray dire, elles ne sont non plus miennes qu'en leur premiere place.
>
> (I. 25. 136c)

Cette métaphore du vol, récurrente dans les *Essais*,[22] souligne bien le plaisir quelque peu coupable de l'esthète, qui finira même par trouver des qualités à une phrase des *Tusculanes*: '...dict Cicero. Je laisse volontiers à cet homme ses mots propres. Irois-je alterer à l'eloquence son parler?' (II. 12. 543c). Montaigne se donne à voir comme l'un des rares connaisseurs de la latinité qui sache 'ruminer' ce 'langage...tout plein et gros d'une vigueur naturelle' (III. 5. 872b et 873b). 'Nous avons bien plus de poëtes, que de juges et interpretes de poësie. Il est plus aisé de la faire, que de la cognoistre' (I. 37. 231c), déplore-t-il au livre I. Rares sont les lecteurs capables de 'remarquer par où un bon autheur se surmonte, par où se rehausse, poisant les mots, les phrases, les inventions une apres l'autre' (III. 8. 937c).

Sans conteste, Montaigne est de ceux-là: chaque citation vient le démontrer; il sait 'poiser' ses emprunts (II. 10. 408c). De ces auteurs qui 'sont tout epigramme' (III. 5. 873b), il a su ne retenir que les passages 'où ils sont les plus roides' (I. 26.148c); mais il se garde bien de les traduire,[23] comme il a fait naguère de la *Théologie naturelle* de Sebond (II. 12. 439-40). Quintilien n'avait-il pas déjà remarqué au sujet des plus grands: 'quantum virtutis habeant, vel hoc ipso cognoscimus, quod imitari non possumus'?[24]

Puisqu'il ne peut rivaliser avec ces poètes, Montaigne se réserve le rôle du rhapsode; et sa paraphrase, au chapitre 37 du livre I, du texte platonicien est transparente: il s'identifie manifestement à Ion, lui qui sait discerner 'la beauté d'une veue ferme et rassise' (I. 37. 231c); et il nous décrit son office: 'La fureur qui espoinçonne celuy qui la sçait penetrer, fiert encores un tiers à la luy ouyr traitter et reciter: comme l'aymant, non seulement attire un' aiguille, mais infond encores en icelle sa faculté d'en attirer d'autres' (I. 37. 232c). Un tel parallèle permet de mieux saisir dans sa vigueur l'image de la couture si souvent employée par Montaigne pour évoquer son activité d'écriture.[25]

Mlle de Gournay, pressée par l'imprimeur de 'tourner les passages Latins des *Essais*' a, elle aussi, été ravie et transportée, fascinée même par le prestige de cette forme:

> Ceste masse ou plutost nuée et moisson d'Autheurs latins est la cresme et la fleur choisie à dessein, comme on void, de l'ouvrage des plus excellents Escrivains, et plus elegans et riches de langage comme d'invention: adjoutons figurez et succincts. Or d'exprimer la conception d'un grand Ouvrier, estoffée de telles qualitez d'élocution, et l'exprimer en une langue inférieure, avec quelque grace, vigueur et briefveté, but d'un pertinent traducteur, ce n'est pas léger effort. Mais combien est-ce d'exprimer près de douze cents passages de ce qualibre, amples, médiocres ou petits?[26]

La longueur de la citation (et certaines ont plus de cinq vers, surtout celles de Lucrèce)[27] n'y fait rien; chacune a une densité, une concision, une *brevitas* qui la rapproche inévitablement du *genus dicendi* élu par Montaigne, 'singulierement beau, sec, bref, signifiant', à l'image de ce Gascon des montagnes, 'nerveux, puissant et pertinent' (II. 17. 639a-c), qui a séduit Montaigne.

Cette analyse, applicable aux vers,[28] vaut-elle pour la prose latine? Reconnaissons-le avec Montaigne, ses 'premiers essays...puent un peu à l'estranger' (III. 5. 875b); ils sont farcis de traductions de Sénèque et de passages de Plutarque — parfois fort étendus — copiés sans vergogne par-dessus l'épaule d'Amyot. Même si l'on suit Montaigne dans l'analyse de son travail de composition, comme nous l'avons fait, il est incontestable que la 'forme' des premiers essais a été étoffée par la traduction, la paraphrase, voire son avatar, l'imitation. Mais l'on ne saurait ignorer les corrections portées en 1588 aux deux premiers livres, qui sont pour beaucoup des ajouts de citations, et surtout les retouches postérieures, qui apportent à elles seules 454 citations nouvelles.[29]

Après 1588 se produit un phénomène minutieusement décrit par Villey;[30] alors que Montaigne n'avait jusque-là cité que des poètes latins — ou presque — il couvre désormais les marges de l'exemplaire de Bordeaux de citations empruntées aux prosateurs, Cicéron, Sénèque ou Tite-Live. On constate par ailleurs un net retour du latin, puisque certains passages — même versifiés — qu'il avait traduits ou imités en vernaculaire dans un premier temps sont, dans les couches B ou C, assortis de leur modèle antique (I. 8. 32a, b; I. 14. 57a, c, a; III. 12. 1055c, b; voir aussi 608 et 159).

Cette nouvelle pratique va-t-elle à l'encontre du projet mis en place avec le troisième livre, de parler de lui 'tout fin seul' (III. 12. 1055b), comme le pensait Villey? Montaigne 'manque-t-il de plus en plus à sa promesse'? Bref, les quatre dernières années marquent-elles un 'retour à la méthode pédante'?[31]

A nos yeux, la question n'est pas là. Si Montaigne cite désormais de la prose latine, c'est qu'il a conscience d'avoir accompli une œuvre — fût-elle composée en prose et en vulgaire — d'être un écrivain au sens plein du terme: son texte peut maintenant soutenir la comparaison avec l'expression antique dont il croyait naguère encore ne pouvoir atteindre la perfection. Ne flétrissait-il pas en 1580, en opposant sa pratique à la leur, 'les escrivains indiscrets de nostre siecle, qui, parmy leurs ouvrages de neant, vont semant des lieux entiers des anciens autheurs pour se faire honneur' (I. 26. 147a)? Il condamnait en fait leur manque de discernement et leur aveuglement sur eux-mêmes, 'car cett'infinie dissemblance de lustres rend un visage si pasle, si terni et si laid à ce qui est leur, qu'ils y perdent beaucoup plus qu'ils n'y gaignent' (*ibidem*).

Cette humilité — même feinte — n'est plus de mise après 1588, puisque Montaigne entreprend lui-même 'à tous coups de [s']esgaler à [ses] larrecins, d'aller pair à pair quand et eux' (I. 26. 147c); il estime

— à la différence de ce peintre croqué par Plutarque — pouvoir faire maintenant 'venir en sa boutique aucun coq naturel' (III. 5. 874b). Plus que l'honneur de l'allégation, plus que le poids d'une autorité, c'est l'*ornatus* que cherche Montaigne à travers la 'meilleure prose ancienne' qu'il 'seme ceans indifferemment pour vers' (III. 9. 995b-c). Une fois sa forme achevée avec les treize essais du livre III, il orne son texte de prose latine car sa pratique et son expérience d'écrivain lui ont révélé à la fois la *virtus* des prosateurs antiques mais aussi la paradoxale grandeur de son *sermo quotidianus*.

A travers l'accumulation des citations — parfois trois ou quatre pour le même passage — la rivalité souhaitée par les théoriciens de l'imitation a changé d'objet; ce n'est plus l'imitateur qui lutte avec son modèle, ce sont les anciens qui combattent entre eux;[33] et Montaigne généralise ainsi la compétition esquissée dès 1572 dans l'essai 'Du jeune Caton' (I. 37. 232a), moyen le meilleur à ses yeux de révéler aux lecteurs les trésors de la latinité.

* * *

Comment 'emprunter la matière' sans 'empirer la forme' (III. 8. 940b)? Voilà une question que Montaigne semble s'être posée tout au long de la rédaction de son œuvre. Et il nous livre, avec ses *Essais*, la résolution du dilemme qu'a affronté tout écrivain de la Renaissance: imiter au risque de perdre son *genius*, ou faire œuvre originale, mais renoncer à un prestigieux héritage.

Amateur de poésie, il a renoncé à composer des vers latins car 'ils accusoient evidemment le poete qu'[il venait] dernierement de lire' (III. 5. 875b). Ayant choisi de s'exprimer en vulgaire avec nonchalance, il a su s'arracher à sa 'condition singeresse et imitatrice' (*ibidem*); il a voulu, nouveau rhapsode, révéler au 'lecteur apprentif' le prestige d'une forme, d'une langue qui sait exprimer plus qu'elle ne dit, sans l'altérer par l'imitation ni en faire de plats centons.

Par ce tour de force, il est parvenu à résoudre la contradiction qui minait le programme de l'Ecole poétique de 1550, et qui n'avait pas échappé à un B. Aneau;[34] il a réussi à composer en français, à être totalement français, tout en 'pillant les sacrez Thesors'[35] des anciens; il a créé l'œuvre à la fois la plus imprégnée de l'Antiquité et la plus prometteuse pour le développement de la littérature vernaculaire. Bref, en subvertissant le processus antique et médiéval de l'allégation et de l'emprunt, il a su concilier l'inconciliable, la similitude et la différence; il a pu être à la fois identique et tout autre.

NOTES

1 Dans le *Ciceronianus* (1528), voir J. Chomarat, *Grammaire et rhétorique chez Erasme* (Paris, 1981), pp. 832-3.

2 G. Defaux ('Rhétorique et représentation dans les *Essais*', in *Rhétorique de Montaigne: actes du colloque de la Société des Amis de Montaigne (Paris, 14 et 15 décembre 1984)*, éd. F. Lestringant (Paris, 1985), pp. 30-2) a déjà montré cette impossibilité pour Montaigne, qui 'semble avoir soigneusement lu' Erasme. (Pour l'influence d'Erasme sur les *Essais*, voir aussi notre contribution *ibidem*, pp. 85-99.)

3 *Ciceronianus*, éd. Gambaro (Brescia, 1965), lignes 1440-1. 'Montaigne cannot *be* Socrates', dit de même T. Cave (*The Cornucopian Text: Problems of Writing in the French Renaissance* (Oxford, 1979), p. 308) qui analyse dans ces pages le refus par Montaigne de l'imitation cicéronienne.

4 *Institutio oratoria*, X. 2. 1.

5 Pour les effets de l'admiration sur l'imitateur voir, outre Quintilien, *Ad Herennium*, IV. 2-8.

6 Scaliger présente par exemple ainsi son imitation latine de la pièce XV d'Anacréon: 'Certat cum Automedonte aut Anacreonte' (*Poemata*, éd. 1574, I. 160). Les humanistes se souviennent des prescriptions de Quintilien (pour qui la paraphrase doit être 'circa eosdem sensus *certamen* atque aemulationem'; *Institutio oratoria*, X. 5. 5) ou de Pline le Jeune (qui recommande à Fuscus de 'interdum et notissima eligere et *certare* cum electis'; *Epistulae* VII. 9. 3).

7 Du Bellay, *Deffence et illustration de la langue françoyse*, I. xii; voir K. Meerhoff, *Rhétorique et poétique au XVIe siècle en France: Du Bellay, Ramus et les autres*, Studies in Medieval and Reformation Thought, 36 (Leyde, 1986), pp. 112-13.

8 T. Cave (*op. cit.*, p. 278) et G. Defaux (*art. cit.*, p. 43) ont déjà souligné l'importance de cette formule érasmienne chez Montaigne.

9 Voir quelques suggestions à ce propos de L. Bote, 'Authenticité, originalité et imitation littéraire chez Montaigne', *BSAM*, 4e série,

XVIII (1969), 13-23.

10 *Deffence et illustration*, I. 7, éd. E. Person (Paris, 1892), p. 69.

11 Et présente dans le *Ciceronianus* (lignes 2539-51, éd. citée)! Sur la fortune de cette métaphore dans l'Antiquité et au XVIe siècle, voir J. von Stackelberg, 'Das Bienengleichnis: ein Beitrag zur Geschichte der literarischen *Imitatio*', *Romanische Forschungen*, LXVIII (1956), 271-93.

12 147a, 378c, 658a, 665-6c, 819c, 1055c. Cette affirmation réitérée de l'inversion du mouvement habituel, qui mène de la lecture à l'écriture, trouve confirmation dans les statistiques dressées par P. Bonnet ('La Source d'une citation latine de Montaigne', *BSAM*, 4e série, XIX (1969), 43-9): sur les 1328 citations des *Essais*, 543 sont apportées en 1588, 454 seront ajoutées sur l'exemplaire de Bordeaux.

13 Voir à ce sujet les analyses très stimulantes de F. Goyet, 'A propos de "ces pastissages de lieux communs": le rôle des notes de lecture dans la genèse des *Essais*', *BSAM*, 7e série, V-VI (1986), 11-26, p. 23.

14 Voir 127a, 146a, 169a, 173a, 231c, 253b, 408c, 873b, 874b.

15 Voir M. Metschies, *Zitat und Zitierkunst in Montaignes Essais* (Genève, 1966); A. Compagnon, *La Seconde Main; ou, le travail de la citation* (Paris, 1979); M. McKinley, *Words in a Corner: Studies in Montaigne's Latin Quotations*, French Forum Monographs, 26 (Lexington, 1981); A. Berthiaume, 'Pratique de la citation dans les *Essais* de Montaigne', *Renaissance et Réformation*, XX (1984), 91-105; C. Blum, 'La Fonction du "déjà dit" dans les *Essais*: emprunter, alléguer, citer', *CAIEF*, XXXIII (1981), 35-51; D. G. Coleman, 'Quelques citations partielles d'Horace dans les *Essais*', in *Montaigne et les Essais 1580-1980: actes du congrès de Bordeaux (juin 1980)*, prés. Pierre Michel (Paris et Genève, 1983), 43-7; A. Dessein, 'Sur quelques citations cachées dans les *Essais*', *BSAM*, 4e série, XIV (1968), 39-41; L. Pertile, 'Su alcune nuove fonti degli *Essais*', *BHR*, XXXI (1969), 481-94; *id.*, 'Noterella sul testo degli *Essais*', *Studi Francesi*, XVI (1972), n° 47-8, 336-8; *id.*, 'Paper and Ink: The Structure of Unpredictability', in *O un Amy! Essays in Honor of D. M. Frame*, French Forum Monographs, 5, éd. R. C. La Charité (Lexington, 1977), 190-218; J. Zimmermann, 'L'Emploi des citations chez Montaigne', *BSAM*, 5e série, XXI (1977), 63-8. Nous n'avons pu consulter la thèse de C.-M. Brousseau-Beuermann, 'La "copie" de Montaigne: étude sur les citations dans les *Essais*', (Harvard, Dissertation Abstracts, XLVII, 2176 A).

16 Préface, éd. 1635 in fol., sig. &&&[r]. Balzac se vantera lui aussi

plus tard d'avoir 'le don d'application' (XXXIX entretien, t. II, p. 512, éd. B. Beugnot (Paris, 1972); voir introduction, pp. xxix et xliii).

17 Tout en soulignant que: 'Ce sont belles armes, mais elles sont mal emmanchées.'

18 Sur cette première citation, emblématique à plus d'un titre, voir l'analyse de M. McKinley, *op. cit.*, pp. 17-20.

19 'La Mise en mots dans la *Délie* de Scève: plaidoyer pour une anabase', in *L'Intelligence du passé: les faits, l'écriture et le sens: Mélanges J. Lafond* (Tours, 1988), 73-85.

20 La citation est souvent introduite dans le corps même d'une phrase pour rompre la chaîne syntaxique ou casser *a posteriori* un rythme trop périodique (94-5, 170, 179, 193 etc.).

21 Montaigne se refuse en effet à enseigner, et il prend avec le choix du style coupé le contre-pied des préceptes de Sénèque: 'facilius tamen insidit, quod exspectatur, quam quod praetervolat. Denique tradere homines discipulis praecepta dicuntur: non traditur quod fugit' (*Epistulae* 40. 3).

22 Voir 651b, 665-6c, 1056c.

23 N'oublions pas que depuis les théoriciens de l'Antiquité (Cicéron, Pline, Quintilien) la traduction était considérée comme une propédeutique nécessaire à l'imitation; voir A. Compagnon, 'Montaigne: de la traduction des autres à la traduction de soi', *Littérature*, LV (1984), 37-44.

24 *Institutio oratoria* X. 5. 8.

25. 'Il n'est subject si vain, qui ne merite un rang en cette rapsodie' (I. 13. 48a). Voir aussi 995b, 1067b (couture); 171c, 576a, 749a (coudre); 148c, 183a, 331a (rapiécer).

26 Préface, éd. cit., sig. &&&ii^{r-v}.

27 La longueur des citations de Lucrèce répond aussi sans doute (voir la communication de D. Ménager ici même) à un désir de mieux faire connaître l'auteur latin, alors peu prisé.

28 Notons aussi que Montaigne ne se contente pas, comme on l'a affirmé trop souvent, de citer les vers et de paraphraser la prose: il juge parfois la poésie latine indigne d'être citée. Ainsi, dans l'*Apologie*, le passage (II. 12. 470a) qui livre le moyen de déterminer quels sont les meilleurs chiots d'une portée est inspiré de Némésien (*Cyné-gétiques*, vv. 147-57) ou de Fracastor (*Alcon*, vv. 60-3).

29 Voir l'article de P. Bonnet cité à la note 12.

30 *Les Sources et l'évolution des 'Essais' de Montaigne*, 2e éd. (Paris,

1933), t. II, pp. 506-34.

31 *Idem, ibidem.*

32 Voir M. Fumaroli, 'Michel de Montaigne; ou, l'éloquence du for intérieur', in *Les Formes brèves de la prose et le discours discontenu (XVIe-XVIIe siècles)*, éd. J. Lafond (Paris, 1984), 27-50.

33 Fait déjà souligné par Villey, *op. cit.*, II, 526. Pour ces 'grappes' de citations, voir 138a-c, 624c, 940b-c.

34 C'est au *Quintil Horatien* que nous avons emprunté notre titre: 'Tu ne fais autre chose par tout l'œuvre...que nous induire a gréciser et latiniser en Françoys' (in éd. Person de la *Deffence et illustration*, p. 194). Pour une bonne analyse du pamphlet et des contradictions qu'il démontre avec clarté, voir K. Meerhoff, *op. cit.*, pp. 135-64.

35 Du Bellay, *Deffence et illustration*, conclusion, p. 162, éd. cit.

Les Citations de Lucrèce chez Montaigne

Daniel Ménager

Une étude des citations de Montaigne se passe aujourd'hui de justifications. Chacun reconnaît l'importance de ces 'parements empruntez' (III. 12. 1055b) dans la poétique du texte. Mais la théorie florissante de la citation a besoin de quelques travaux pratiques, analogues à celui de Mary McKinley sur les emprunts de Montaigne à Horace, Ovide, et Virgile.[1] J'ai choisi Lucrèce parce qu'il vient juste après Horace dans le tableau de fréquence de Villey (149 citations)[2] mais surtout en raison des avantages qu'il présente. 'Philosophus et poeta', comme le présentent les titres de certaines éditions du seizième siècle,[3] il échappe de plus en plus, en cet automne de la Renaissance, aux condamnations sommaires qui le frappaient pour son matérialisme.[4] Voici que peu à peu il incarne une morale vénérable, celle d'Epicure, dont certains aspects sont acceptables par la tradition. Montaigne lui-même illustre ce mouvement, lui qui fait trois emprunts au *De natura rerum* pour les inscriptions de sa 'librairie', le thème de l'une d'entre elles n'étant autre que l'aveuglement des hommes dont parle aussi l'amère sagesse de l'Ecclésiaste.[5] Quant à la poésie de Lucrèce, elle suscite l'admiration d'un grand nombre et en particulier de Lambin dont Montaigne utilise l'édition parue en 1563.[6] Poète à la fois élégant et archaïque, il est capable de plaire aux cicéroniens comme aux tenants de la *prisca philosophia*.

Quel sera donc le choix de Montaigne: Lucrèce philosophe ou Lucrèce poète? De quelle philosophie s'agit-il dans le premier cas? De quelle poésie dans le second? A moins que Montaigne ne découvre un autre Lucrèce, l'un des plus originaux de la Renaissance, un poète qui reprend les questions là où les laisse la philosophie, avec pour seule guide la force de son imagination.

LES CITATIONS DE LUCRECE CHEZ MONTAIGNE

* * *

Il n'est guère dans les habitudes de Montaigne de commenter ses citations. L'exemple qui confirme la règle se trouve dans le célèbre chapitre 5 du livre III, 'Sur des vers de Virgile'. C'est ailleurs et d'une façon détournée que l'auteur des *Essais* formule un certain nombre de jugements sur l'auteur latin. Ainsi dans ce passage de II. 12. 459 où un collage bien particulier réunit une citation-résumé de l'Ecclésiaste (9. 3) et une citation textuelle de Lucrèce. Après l'opinion du 'sage', pour qui 'tout ce qui est sous le Ciel...court une loy et fortune pareille', vient le vers de Lucrèce emprunté au livre V (876): 'Indupedita suis fatalibus omnia vinclis.' Mais du même coup Lucrèce ne devient-il pas lui aussi un Sage puisqu'il dit la même chose que l'Ecclésiaste? Ainsi se confirme l'intégration du penseur latin dans la tradition, ce qui était déjà la clé de sa 'cohabitation' avec l'auteur sacré sur les poutres de la librairie. C'est un éloge plus neuf, et aussi plus fort, qui est décerné à Lucrèce, toujours d'une manière oblique, dans un autre passage de *l'Apologie de Raimond Sebond*. Montaigne vient de citer deux vers sur la pluralité des mondes, l'une des thèses encore combattues du *De natura rerum*, et c'est pour enchaîner: 'Les plus fameux esprits du temps passé l'ont creue' (II. 12. 524a). Comment Lucrèce, à la faveur de cette présentation, ne serait-il pas l'un d'entre eux?

Lucrèce philosophe, donc, mais philosophe fragile: c'est ce que dit très clairement cette fois un autre passage de II. 12, où Montaigne cite quelques vers du second éloge d'Epicure (V. 8 sqq.), celui où Lucrèce exprime sa reconnaissance à l'égard du philosophe athénien 'per artem / Fluctibus è tantis vitam tantisque tenebris / In tam tranquillo et tam clara luce locavit' (489a). Voici le commentaire: 'paroles tres-magnifiques et belles; mais un bien legier accident mist l'entendement de cettuy-cy en pire estat que celuy du moindre bergier, nonobstant ce Dieu præcepteur et cette divine sapience': allusion à la folie de Lucrèce 'rendu insensé', comme le précise un autre passage en conformité avec la tradition, 'par un breuvage amoureux' (II. 2. 345a). On a noté avec raison la façon ironique dont la sagesse la plus haute était humiliée par la vie. Mais ce n'est peut-être qu'une manière de lire. Qui ne sait que pour Montaigne la folie n'est pas loin des plus 'gaillardes elevations d'un esprit' (II. 12. 492a)?[7] Le thème de la folie de Lucrèce, que Lambin ne reprenait pas et qui, dans la biographie de Crinitus, était la fureur de l'inspiré,[8] consacre à la fois la faiblesse et la grandeur de l'écrivain latin.

Peu de jugements donc, et quand il s'en trouve, des jugements ambigus. Il en va souvent de même en ce qui concerne la façon dont sont présentées certaines idées du philosophe. Le mieux sera de s'en tenir à celles qui ont provoqué les réactions les plus indignées: la pluralité des mondes et la nature mortelle de l'âme. La première, on l'a dit, doit une partie de son prestige au fait que 'les plus fameux esprits du temps passé l'ont creue' (II. 12. 524a). On est loin ici de l'indignation de Ronsard contre ce qu'il appelle une 'fureur'.[9] Encore faut-il préciser que pour Montaigne cette idée est de l'ordre du possible: l'affirmer comme une certitude serait retomber dans le dogmatisme. Beaucoup plus intéressant est l'exposé concernant la nature de l'âme. Il appartient à l'une des nombreuses doxographies de l'*Apologie* dont le sens dépend, en grande partie, des modalités de l'énonciation. D'où l'importance des emprunts. Trois pages (549-52) résument l'opinion des philosophes anciens favorables aux idées de Démocrite et d'Epicure, trois pages nourries pour ne pas dire truffées de citations de Lucrèce, presque toutes ajoutées en 1588, et qui illustrent la fragilité de l'âme sensible à tous les maux du corps. Parmi celles-ci, une place à part est à faire aux vers 175-6 du livre III, à ce fameux 'corpoream naturam animi esse necesse est' qui paraissait si choquant à Lambin qu'il le jugeait interpolé.[10] Montaigne les cite sans condamner l'idée. Pourquoi le ferait-il puisqu'il résume les idées des autres? Lambin avait déjà fait confiance au lecteur du poème pour savoir distinguer le bon grain de l'ivraie.[11] Mais la présentation elle-même ne possède pas toujours la froide objectivité d'une doxographie et l'on se demande parfois si le regard de Lucrèce sur l'âme n'est pas un peu celui de Montaigne, d'autant plus que le style indirect utilisé ici associe le discours de l'un aux observations des autres. Lucrèce n'est pas seulement présent, dans cette page, grâce aux citations faites de son œuvre: il en est plus ou moins la source et cela, une nouvelle fois, grâce à l'épisode légendaire de sa folie. Il y a gros à parier que c'est à lui que songe Montaigne lorsqu'il évoque cet 'inconvenient où, chez un philosophe, une ame devient l'ame d'un fol, troublée, renversée et perdue' (II. 12. 551a). Inconvénient: sans doute, mais aussi quelle conformité étonnante entre la vie du philosophe et l'une des thèses de son œuvre: comme si la première signait la seconde.

Autant dire, du même coup, que Montaigne se sépare de son auteur chaque fois qu'il tombe dans le dogmatisme et sans trop se soucier de savoir si celui-ci est imputable à Epicure ou à son disciple. C'est par exemple un signe de la 'vanité de l'humaine raison' que de ne pouvoir imaginer l'union de l'âme immortelle et du corps mortel. Ici une citation de Lucrèce (551a) sert à le condamner. Le cas pourtant est relativement rare, et c'est à des approbations apparentes que revient la place donnée à Lucrèce dans deux prosopopées fameuses des *Essais*: celles de la raison en II. 12; celle de la nature en I. 20.[12] La première, adressée à Platon, ne comporte pas moins de cinq citations de Lucrèce: treize vers au total, en deux pages, empruntés à un passage-clé du poème, celui du livre III où le philosophe réfute l'idée d'une survie de l'âme.[13] L'artifice rhétorique de la prosopopée donne un poids singulier, en principe, aux paroles de Lucrèce puisque c'est maintenant la raison elle-même qui parle à travers lui, ce qui fausse le dialogue avec Platon réduit à ses seules idées. Il n'est pas sûr pourtant que Lucrèce sorte gagnant de cette joute philosophique. En étudiant les prosopopées ironiques des *Essais*, A. Tournon a montré en effet que le discours de la raison, après l'avoir emporté sur Platon, se trouvait lui-même dévalué 'par référence implicite à l'orthodoxie chrétienne': 'aux démonstrations de la raison est simplement opposée une fin de non-recevoir.'[14] Le tort de la prosopopée est de substituer une instance impersonnelle et impressionnante à l'humble discours de l'individu.

L'autre prosopopée, qui comprend une vingtaine de vers de Lucrèce, a ceci de particulier qu'elle puise une partie de ceux-ci dans ce qui est déjà chez lui une prosopopée: figure de rhétorique à laquelle le philosophe a recours pour mettre un terme aux plaintes de l'homme devant la mort.[15] La philosophie se réfugie dans la rhétorique pour enlever l'adhésion du lecteur. C'est un peu ce qui se passe aussi chez Montaigne qui n'en fait pas ici un usage ironique, se bornant à ratifier son discours *in fine* par une réflexion à la première personne. La voix de la Nature reste vénérable et Montaigne a étoffé son exhortation d'autres citations lucrétiennes, choisissant les vers les plus capables de toucher la sensibilité de l'homme: c'est le début du livre II (vv. 76 et 79) qui fournit par exemple l'image déjà plus ou moins proverbiale des générations humaines se transmettant le flambeau de la vie (I. 20. 92b). Mais quel crédit accorder à une philosophie qui use si habilement de la rhétorique et qui en impose peut-être grâce à elle? La présence de Lucrèce dans ces prosopopées révèle à la fois la fascination éprouvée par Montaigne devant sa philosophie et la distance qu'il est tenté de prendre vis-à-vis d'elle.

Plus qu'un double de Montaigne, Lucrèce est en fait l'un de ses interlocuteurs privilégiés. On en trouvera la preuve dans un passage qui figure au début de l'*Apologie* et qui concerne encore la mort. Montaigne vient d'écrire que si nous accordions aux 'promesses de la beatitude eternelle' autant de crédit qu'à un 'discours philosophique', nous quitterions la vie avec la même facilité qu'un serpent quitte sa peau ou un cerf devenu vieux ses cornes trop longues (II. 12. 445a). Ces images sont de Lucrèce; elles figurent dans trois vers du poète (III. 612-14) ajoutés en 1588. La proposition principale se poursuit avec un emprunt à Paul (Philippiens 1. 23): 'Je veuil estre dissout, dirions nous, et estre aveques Jesus-Christ.'[16] Tout serait limpide si les trois vers de Lucrèce n'étaient pas la conclusion d'un raisonnement très différent: si notre âme était immortelle, nous quitterions la vie dans la joie! Montaigne exclut cet irréel du présent au profit d'un autre. Mais qui peut assurer que les vers exclus ne laissent pas une trace dans le texte? Ne pourrait-on même dire que le 'discours philosophique' auquel Montaigne fait allusion pour noter son excessive autorité est un peu celui de Lucrèce, et que la citation elle-même est la preuve de cette autorité puisque les vers du philosophe 'athée' servent à dire la croyance en la vie éternelle?

Interlocuteur privilégié donc, à condition qu'il ne tombe pas lui-même dans le dogmatisme. Il est révélateur que le seul éloge d'Epicure repris sans ironie dans les *Essais*, sur les trois que compte le poème, soit celui du livre VI, où Lucrèce ne campe plus son idole dans la pose avantageuse du conquérant de la nature, mais dans celle plus humble du moraliste ému par la misère humaine. Neuf vers de cet éloge, ajoutés en 1588, figurent au chapitre 'D'un mot de Cæsar' (I. 53. 309-10b). Mais même dans ce cas l'éloge ne s'intègre pas vraiment au discours de Montaigne, et la syntaxe ne sait trop quoi en faire. Témoin d'une double admiration: celle de Lucrèce pour Epicure, et celle de Montaigne pour Lucrèce, ce passage révèle une sorte de non-coïncidence: de même que Lucrèce n'est pas parvenu à s'identifier avec le philosophe athénien, de même Montaigne ne se confond pas avec Lucrèce, qu'il admire. Dans cette béance se joue sa liberté.

* * *

Lucrèce s'est efforcé à la philosophie, mais il était d'abord Poète: c'est très exactement ce que nous dit cette phrase de II. 2 déjà rencontrée: 'Lucrèce, *ce grand poëte*, a beau Philosopher et se bander, la voylà rendu insensé par un breuvage amoureux' (345a). La contention philoso-phique, aussi grande chez les épicuriens que chez les stoïciens, n'assure pas à l'individu la maîtrise de sa propre vie, dominée par sa sensibilité, surtout s'il est poète.

C'est donc tout naturellement en compagnie des plus grands poètes que Lucrèce apparaît dans le chapitre 'Des livres' (II. 10): Virgile, Catulle, et Horace (410a). A une époque qui sacralise Virgile (que l'on songe, par exemple, à Scaliger et Ronsard),[17] Montaigne ne récuse pas l'idée qu'on puisse lui comparer Lucrèce: 'Je suis d'opinion que c'est à la verité une comparaison inegale; mais j'ay bien à faire à me r'asseurer en cette creance, quand je me treuve attaché à quelque beau lieu de ceux de Lucrece' (411a). Celui-ci compte en effet, on l'a dit, de chauds partisans et Lambin est l'un d'entre eux qui ne tarit pas d'éloges sur le style du poète latin 'gravis, copiosus, amplus, magnificus, elatus, ornatus';[18] d'autant plus 'ornatus' peut-être que selon une tradition vivante encore au seizième siècle, Cicéron aurait poli l'ouvrage un peu rugueux laissé par Lucrèce à sa mort.[19] Il n'est pas facile de savoir quelles étaient pour Montaigne les qualités proprement stylistiques de Lucrèce car le fameux commentaire de III. 5 réunit dans un même mouvement d'admiration le style de Virgile et celui de son devancier: c'est l'un et l'autre qui possèdent ce langage 'tout plein et gros d'une vigueur naturelle et constante' et qui sont 'tout epigramme' (III. 5. 873b). L'auteur de l'*Enéide* comme celui du *De natura rerum* illustrent une conception du style en général qui condamne l'afféterie au profit de la vigueur et le culte de la forme au profit de la force. La poésie de Lucrèce possède aussi cette qualité de ne jamais être obscure tout en étant philosophique: c'est l'idée qu'introduit d'une façon indirecte la condamnation de l'obscurité d'Héraclite par Lucrèce lui-même.

30

Une approche purement stylistique du poème de Lucrèce ne tente pourtant pas Montaigne dans la mesure où il lui paraît impossible de distinguer la forme et la pensée: 'C'est la gaillardise de l'imagination qui esleve et enfle les parolles' (III. 5. 873b). Ce qui est vrai en revanche, c'est que l'imagination du poète échappe parfois au contrôle de sa philosophie, et Montaigne prend un malin plaisir à laisser parler, dans ses citations, la folle du logis. On voudrait le montrer d'abord à propos de celle de III. 5, qu'on rapprochera de quelques autres passages concernant aussi l'amour.[20] Ce qui en effet mérite d'être relevé, ce n'est pas que Montaigne ait été sensible à la description de la 'jouissance desrobée' de Mars et de Vénus (872b), mais bien, comme l'a noté Philip Hendrick, la manière dont la citation déforme le sens du passage. Chargés d'illustrer avec un exemple frappant l'ataraxie des épicuriens, les vers retenus par Montaigne évoquent surtout le plaisir des sens et la joie de la passion: la citation est coupée au moment même où le poète latin demandait pour les Romains le calme de la paix ('placidam pacem'). Rien de moins paisible que cette description amoureuse où les verbes sont plus nombreux que les noms et les adjectifs: sur les cinq mots venant de Lucrèce repris ensuite dans le commentaire, trois sont des verbes conjugués, les deux autres étant des formes verbales. Le découpage même des vers en question révèle l'influence d'une autre citation, celle des vers de Virgile. Comme l'a récemment observé Mary McKinley, dans l'*Enéide* (VIII. 389), Vénus use de sa séduction pour convaincre Vulcain de forger des armes pour Enée, donc pour lui permettre de continuer la guerre.[21] Chez l'un, l'amour est un chemin vers la paix; chez l'autre il mène à la guerre. Le souvenir des vers de Virgile infléchit donc l'usage qui est fait de ceux de Lucrèce, mouvement exactement inverse de celui de l'histoire littéraire où c'est Virgile qui s'est souvenu de Lucrèce. L'essentiel reste que Montaigne libère la poésie du contrôle de la philosophie.

Que dire aussi de deux autres vers de Lucrèce sur l'étreinte amoureuse (IV. 1106-7) si bien intégrés en II. 11 au discours de Montaigne qu'ils semblent venir de lui, de cette évocation frémissante de la joie des corps ('Atque in eo est venus ut muliebria conserat arva', II. 11. 429-30) qui enlève toute force à 'nostre discours'. Ce 'nous' range aussi l'auteur parmi les victimes consentantes de l'amour dont Lucrèce parle si bien qu'on peut se demander si, comme cela arrive parfois dans des traités de morale, il n'amène pas à lui ceux qu'il croit en détourner. Nouvelle défaite de la philosophie consommée dans la syntaxe même de la phrase: le discours connaît lui aussi une sorte de ravissement dont le phénomène de la citation porte témoignage. Double plaisir: dans l'amour qui transporte et dans la citation qui déporte, mais si bien contrôlée que Montaigne communie avec son poète.

Le plaisir ainsi pris aux vers de Lucrèce n'a plus besoin d'être justifié. Il arrive même que la séduction soit si forte que Montaigne cite ce qu'il condamne. C'est ainsi qu'on peut comprendre le sort qui est fait au passage célèbre qui décrit la condition misérable de l'enfant à sa naissance comparée à celle des animaux.[22] Ces vers qui permettaient au poète latin de nier l'idée même de Providence divine, illustrent pour Montaigne une idée erronée: 'il y a en la police du monde une esgalité plus grande et une relation plus uniforme' (II. 12. 456a). La Nature s'occupe de toutes ses créatures, des hommes comme des animaux. Il faut donc rejeter 'ces plaintes là' qui sont 'fauces'. Elles sont aussi 'vulgaires' parce qu'on les trouve partout et notamment dans la topique de la *miseria hominis* qui se nourrit de Pline (*Historia naturalis*, début du livre VII) et du pessimisme médiéval.[23] Si 'ces plaintes là' sont à la fois 'fauces' et 'vulgaires', pourquoi quatorze vers de Lucrèce, rajoutés en 1588? Cette page de l'*Apologie* combine une fois de plus la citation-résumé et la citation textuelle. La première s'appuie sur le *locus* classique de Pline pour démontrer la nudité de l'homme. Voilà ce qui est 'vulgaire'. Mais Lucrèce ne l'est pas car il ajoute à ce *topos* une note pathétique qui lui appartient en propre. Faux peut-être, mais non vulgaire. Et Montaigne ne se demande pas s'il est prudent de donner tant de lustre à l'erreur. L'image du *puer nudus* fait écho en lui à une profonde inquiétude dont il a bien du mal à se délivrer. La citation lucrétienne révèle la complexité de l'auteur des *Essais*. Sa force a été de s'imposer à lui malgré la thèse qu'il défend.

* * *

Il y a donc — les signes en sont multiples — un plaisir à Lucrèce, un plaisir qui échappe aux catégories du vrai et du faux qui sont celles de la philosophie. Mais Montaigne ne serait pas fidèle à lui-même si ce plaisir n'était aussi celui de la réflexion. La poésie de Lucrèce donne toujours à penser. C'est pourquoi elle est philosophique. Un autre Lucrèce se découvre alors dont Montaigne redéfinit l'allégeance à la philosophie d'Epicure. A plusieurs reprises, l'auteur des *Essais* se sert du disciple contre le maître: à propos par exemple des opinions de celui-ci concernant les dieux: c'est Lucrèce qui condamne les représentations marquées par l'anthropomorphisme.[24] Mais point n'est besoin, souvent, d'une dialectique aussi retorse. C'est l'épicurisme lui-même que l'*Apologie* propose de repenser, comme l'a bien montré A. Tournon. Quand Montaigne écrit qu'il ne se persuade pas 'aysement qu'Epicurus, Platon et Pythagoras nous ayent donné pour argent contant leurs Atomes, leurs Idées et leurs Nombres', il découvre sous leur dogmatisme un pyrrhonisme secret (II. 12. 511a). Il serait ainsi prêt à 'enrôler tous les philosophes dans la secte de Pyrrhon'.[25] Mais ce n'est pas un jeu comme on pourrait le croire. L'*Apologie* cite largement le passage où Lucrèce affirme qu'il faut soutenir coûte que coûte la thèse de la certitude des sens,[26] faute de quoi 'notre vie elle-même tomberait en ruines' et nous ne saurions plus à quoi nous fier pour éviter les précipices qui la bordent. 'Ce conseil desesperé et si peu philosophique', comme l'appelle Montaigne (II. 12. 592c), révèle l'angoisse d'un homme qui doute et qui avoue son doute. La poésie sera chargée non de cacher la misère de la philosophie, mais d'aller, si possible, plus loin d'elle.

Voilà qui donne sens à la 'plaisante et subtile apparence' (II. 12. 511a) de certaines rêveries philosophiques. Remarquons en passant que le vocabulaire employé est maintenant celui de la rhétorique, auxiliaire de la poésie dans sa volonté d'exploration du monde. Là se situe l'usage le plus personnel de Lucrèce par Montaigne. Nous en prendrons deux exemples. Celui du langage des animaux d'abord: question abordée en II. 12 pour combattre l'orgueil de l'homme. Aristote,[27] sans doute par l'intermédiaire de Laurent Joubert,[28] fournit un certain nombre d'arguments à l'appui de l'idée que les bêtes communiquent entre elles et selon des modalités variées. Quatre citations de Lucrèce, empruntées au livre V (vv. 1028-90) viennent cependant ponctuer la réflexion de Montaigne, la dernière (459b) étant un montage de plusieurs vers sur les différents cris des animaux. Le plus étonnant est la manière dont elle est introduite: 'Aristote allegue à ce propos le chant divers des perdris, selon la situation des lieux' (459a). On s'attend à une citation du philosophe grec, mais ce qui vient ce sont les vers de Lucrèce. Le poète se substitue au 'dieu de la science scolastique', alors même qu'ils disent la même chose. Mais une citation d'Aristote aurait eu un effet dogmatique. On ne peut mieux justifier la distinction faite par Montaigne lui-même et reprise par la critique entre l'allégation, 'paraphrase en français du texte grec ou latin' accompagné du nom de l'auteur, et la citation qui fait place, sans le nommer, aux mots du poète.[29] Ce que celui-ci respecte plus que le philosophe, c'est le mystère de la nature. Voilà pourquoi il a sa place ici.

Le second exemple rapproche l'homme de l'animal dans ce territoire qu'ils ont en commun: le rêve. Il semble bien que Montaigne ait été vivement frappé par les quelque soixante vers que Lucrèce lui consacre au livre IV.[30] Il se souvient d'abord (I. 21, 'De la force de l'imagination') du passage concernant le rêve érotique et ce qu'on appelle la 'pollution nocturne' (98a): ce n'est pas l'exemple le plus significatif car les livres de morale devaient le retenir. Assez curieuse est la manière dont deux autres vers sur le rêve trouvent place dans le chapitre sur les 'Coustumes anciennes' (I. 49): il s'agit d'illustrer l'erreur de ceux qui, dans leurs rêves, croient se trouver près d'un urinoir (298a)! C'est encore l'*Apologie* (482a) qui accueille le plus généreusement le texte de Lucrèce: en une page, quatorze vers sont cités, décrivant les rêves des chevaux, des lévriers, et des chiens de garde; tout un développement que Montaigne a morcelé pour la clarté de sa démonstration mais aussi pour mieux accompagner la citation grâce aux expressions fameuses du 'lievre sans poil et sans os' et du 'son de tabourin sans bruict' (481a). Jamais l'osmose entre son texte et celui du poète latin n'a été aussi grande: le 'videbis' de Lucrèce à son lecteur est maintenant lancé à celui des *Essais* pour qu'il observe mieux ce qui l'entoure et notamment cette 'merveille' du rêve des animaux. Et ce sont sans doute ces 'inania.../Cervorum simulachra' qui engendrent les expressions que nous venons de citer. 'Images illusoires' que celles du lièvre endormi mais qui donnent naissance à d'autres images que l'on peut, à la rigueur, appeler aussi 'simulachra': celles de la poésie, tout aussi vaines et tout aussi vraies, simulacres sur des simulacres.[31]

Le propre de cette poésie philosophique, c'est qu'elle n'est pas dupe d'elle-même: elle ne prend pas 'pour argent contant' ce qu'elle dit. Elle explore le rêve comme cette part d'inconnu que les bêtes portent en eux.

Cela signifie aussi que l'admiration n'empêche pas la plus grande liberté dans l'usage qui est fait de ces vers. On voit alors Montaigne entrer dans un véritable dialogue avec celui qu'il cite. Une des descriptions les plus frappantes de Lucrèce (III. 487-91) est celle de l'homme atteint du 'mal caduc', ou si l'on préfère, du 'haut mal': image même de la souffrance de l'âme mêlée au corps et dont elle partage la fortune. Insérée dans le chapitre 'De l'exercitation' (II. 6. 374), mais seulement en 1588, elle fait partie d'un discours qui tente d'établir que ceux qui sont évanouis, proches de leur fin ou victimes d'un accès d'épilepsie, contrairement à ce qu'on croit et qu'a soutenu La Boétie, ne souffrent pas. On perçoit dans cette citation l'écho d'une discussion avec l'ami, discussion qu'alimentent aussi les vers de Lucrèce dont Montaigne fait un usage si paradoxal. Mieux que personne, le poète-philosophe a su décrire la victime du 'mal caduc'. Reste à savoir si elle souffre autant qu'il l'a dit. La citation permet un dialogue intérieur qui ne sera sans doute jamais achevé.

Cette lecture de Lucrèce possède autant d'allure que de liberté. Je citerai pour terminer la manière dont Montaigne utilise le fameux 'suave mari magno' du prologue du livre II. 'Il est doux', écrivait le poète, 'quand sur la vaste mer les vents soulèvent les flots, d'assister de la terre aux rudes épreuves d'autrui: non que la souffrance de personne nous soit un plaisir si grand; mais voir à quels maux on échappe soi-même est chose douce.' Dans le premier chapitre du livre III, Montaigne ignore délibérément la correction, ou plutôt la dénégation du vers 3. Il la transforme en affirmation et les images de Lucrèce servent maintenant à illustrer la nature complexe des sentiments de l'homme devant les malheurs d'autrui et cette 'poincte de volupté maligne' à le voir souffrir (III. 1. 791b). Comme si finalement Lucrèce avait hésité devant l'audace de son intuition, Montaigne la relaie et lui donne toute sa portée.[32]

* * *

On aura peut-être montré la place singulière du texte de Lucrèce dans les *Essais*. Un Lucrèce qui ne ressemble pas à celui qu'inventent à la même époque les humanistes de la dernière Renaissance. Montaigne ne demande aucune révélation au 'poeta vetustissimus', pas plus qu'il ne fait de lui l'incarnation de la sérénité épicurienne. Place singulière aussi par rapport aux autres poètes cités dans les *Essais*, car plus qu'un autre, Lucrèce donne à penser, et cette pensée est inséparable des mots du poème qu'il faut donc citer littéralement. S'il ne s'agissait que de s'approprier, en certains cas, la pensée de l'auteur latin, les mots n'auraient guère d'importance. Mais on ne pourra jamais résumer, par exemple, le 'suave mari magno', dont l'épaisseur même fait sens et qui resurgit sans doute ailleurs. Car si le phénomène de la citation distingue à première vue ce qui est de lui et ce qui est des autres, en fait, comme l'écrit Antoine Compagnon, 'tout se mêle'. Les mots du poète devenu fou sont toujours et en même temps ne sont pas ceux du gentilhomme sage.

NOTES

1 *Words in a Corner: Studies in Montaigne's Latin Quotations*, French Forum Monographs, 26 (Lexington, 1981).

2 48 citations viennent de l'édition de 1580; 3 de celle de 1582; 97 datent de 1588; une seule provient de l'exemplaire de Bordeaux. Une étude d'ensemble, à ce jour, sur Montaigne et Lucrèce: celle de S. Fraisse, *L'Influence de Lucrèce en France au seizième siècle* (Paris, 1962), pp. 170 sqq. Deux articles s'intéressent à la place de Lucrèce dans l'*Apologie*: Philip Hendrick, 'Lucretius in the *Apologie de Raimond Sebond*', *BHR*, XXXVII (1975), 475-66; et G. Ferreyrolles, 'Les Citations de Lucrèce dans l'*Apologie de Raimond Sebond*', *BSAM*, 5ᵉ série, XVII (1976), 49-63. Voir aussi W. G. Moore, 'Lucretius and Montaigne', *Yale French Studies*, XXXVIII (1967), 109-14, article que nous n'avons pu consulter.

3 Par exemple l'édition Gryphe (Lyon, 1540): *T. Cari Lucretii Poetae ac philosophi vetustissimi De Rerum Natura libri sex.*

4 C'est en particulier l'édition de Lambin (1563) qui oppère ce changement: voir S. Fraisse, *op. cit.*, pp. 54 sqq. et J. Jehasse, *La Renaissance de la critique*, Publications de l'Université de Saint Etienne (Saint Etienne, 1976), pp. 90 sqq. Lambin juge encore opportun de désolidariser le poète latin de son maître Epicure, ce que feront d'autres éditeurs: voir M. Bollack, *La Raison de Lucrèce: constitution d'une poétique philosophique avec un essai d'interprétation de la critique lucrétienne* (Paris, 1978). Mais dans la seconde

moitié du seizième siècle, c'est à peine nécessaire, tant l'épicurisme jouit d'une opinion favorable: voir J. Jehasse, *op. cit.*, p. 90.

5 Lucrèce II. 14; *Essais*, p. LXVIII.

6 Voir P. Villey, *Les Sources et l'évolution des Essais de Montaigne* (Paris, 1908), 2 t., I. 169-70.

7 Voir à ce sujet M. Screech, *Montaigne and Melancholy : The Wisdom of the Essays* (London, 1983), p. 46.

8 La *Vie de Lucrèce* par Crinitus, qui figure dans l'édition Gryphe, mentionne cette folie en citant le témoignage d'Eusèbe. Elle aurait été consécutive à l'absorption d'un philtre amoureux ('assumpto amatorio poculo') et l'aurait conduit au suicide (voir Jérôme, *Chronique* in *Opera, Patrologia Latina*, t. XXVII, col. 524-5). On retrouve cette tradition dans les *Historiae poetarum* de Giraldi (Bâle, 1545).

9 *Hymne du Ciel*, in éd. Laumonier, VIII. 147. 92.

10 Ed. cit., p. 203.

11 'Nam quemadmodum apes ex singulis floribus, quod est ad mel conficiendum utilissimum atque aptissimum libare ac depasci consueverunt, quod est inutile non attingunt, aut certe non degustant, ita...' (épître à Charles IX).

12 Respectivement pp. 518-19, et pp. 92-6.

13 *De natura rerum* III. 548-1094.

14 'Les Prosopopées ironiques dans les *Essais*', in *Rhétorique de Montaigne: actes du colloque de la Société des Amis de Montaigne (Paris, 14 et 15 décembre 1984)*, éd. F. Lestringant (Paris, 1985), p. 118.

15 *De natura rerum* III. 741-978.

16 Selon M. Screech (*op. cit.*, p. 46) le lien entre les deux citations se fait par l'intermédiaire du verbe *dissolvi*. Il note également que le passage de Paul n'a pas le statut de citation, Montaigne supposant que le lecteur reconnaîtra l'origine de l'énoncé.

17 Celui, du moins, de la seconde préface de la *Franciade*, publiée en 1587, et qui subit d'ailleurs l'influence de Scaliger.

18 *Préface* à Charles IX.

19 On la trouve par exemple dans la *Vie de Lucrèce* par Crinitus: 'Neque desunt qui scribunt fuisse Lucretii opus a M. Tullio emendatum' (éd. Gryphe, Lyon, 1540) et dans les *Historiae poetarum* de Giraldi, p. 429. Cette tradition remonte à Jérôme. Il est sûr en tout cas que Cicéron admirait le poème de Lucrèce (*Epistulae ad Quintum fratrem* II. 11. 5).

20 *De natura rerum* I. 32-40. Montaigne ne reprend pas le vers 35: 'Atque ita suspiciens tereti cervice reposta.'

21 *Op. cit.*, p. 90.

22 *De natura rerum* V. 222-34.

23 Voir par exemple le *Théâtre du monde (1558)*, de Pierre Boaistuau, éd. M. Simonin (Genève, 1981), p. 74 et l'annotation.

24 II. 12. 517. Montaigne utilise pour cette critique Lucrèce, V. 122-3. Voir G. Ferreyrolles, *art. cit.*, p. 54.

25 A. Tournon, *Montaigne: la glose et l'essai*, (Lyon, 1983), p. 247.

26 *De natura rerum* IV. 499-510.

27 *De generatione animalium* V. 7.

28 *Les Erreurs populaires au fait de la médecine* ont été éditées à Bordeaux, chez S. Millanges, en 1578. Montaigne possède cette édition ou la réimpression de 1579: voir Villey, *Les Sources et l'évolution*, I. 153-4.

29 A. Compagnon, *La Seconde Main; ou, le travail de la citation* (Paris, 1979), p. 292.

30 Vers 962-1036.

31 Montaigne traite aussi du songe et des propos que l'on tient en rêvant dans un passage, II. 5. 367-8, qui cite Lucrèce, V. 1158-1160.

32 Voir sur ce thème le bel article de M. Delon, 'Naufrages vus de loin: les développements narratifs d'un thème lucrétien', *Rivista di letterature moderne e comparate*, XLI, fasc. 2 (1988).

4

Montaigne: Some Classical Notions in their Contexts

M. A. Screech

The greatest single problem which has arisen in my lifetime for those who have the pleasure of teaching those Renaissance authors who have something to say is the virtual extinction among our undergraduates (and among many post-graduates) of a certain kind of knowledge of the past. It is tempting to overstate the scholarly equipment of our generations of students during and after the Second World War: not all of us were fertile fields waiting to bloom. Many were arid deserts resisting any kind of irrigation. But all (in England anyway) had studied enough Latin to be at least vaguely aware of the fact when Montaigne was using French words with Latin meanings or with Latin nuances. Moreover a great deal of theology had entered even unwilling minds through hymn-singing during 'assembly'. And at least some knowledge of the Bible had been instilled by the teaching of 'Religious Knowledge'.

Under these circumstances it was comparatively easy to encourage us readers of Montaigne to be on the alert for many kinds of appreciation of meaning which now require to be pointed out and explained by detailed teaching and patient explanation. Four of those kinds of meaning are briefly mentioned here, with a few examples: 1) the general Latin context of Montaigne's language and thought; 2) classical allusions in classical contexts; 3) classical allusions in contemporary Christian contexts; 4) classical allusions in contemporary political contexts.

* * *

The Latin Context of Montaigne's Language and Thought

The truisms that Montaigne spoke Latin before French, and that standard French was most decidedly not the local language of Montaigne, Toulouse or even Bordeaux, make the *a priori* acceptance of Latin usages in the *Essais* easy to convey. It is the detail which causes the problem, since in this case not only every word has its history but the same word used in different contexts may have several different histories. A modern reader coming across the term *guerre sociale* in the chapter 'De l'incertitude de nostre jugement' (I. 47. 282a) can hardly be expected to know that *bellum sociale* means the war of the 'confederates' or 'allies' (that being the classical meaning of *socialis*, from *socius*, 'ally') and that even in English the 'Social Wars' used to mean primarily the wars between Rome and her Italian allies (90-89 B.C.) and then 'Civil' wars generally, including our own and the Religious Wars in France. Here the context is important in that those more modern wars were seen by contemporaries, at least in part, in the light of Roman precedent when they used the Latinate term *social* for them.

Sometimes the lack of awareness of a Latin context can lead to puzzlement or complete misunderstanding. Take for example the statement in 'De l'incommodité de la grandeur':

> Homere a esté contrainct de consentir que Venus fut blessée au combat de Troye, une si douce saincte, et si delicate...
>
> (III. 7. 918-19b)

What a stumbling-block that word 'saincte' is: Venus, a saint! (For those who already find Montaigne's Catholicism puzzling, here is real σκάνδαλον!) But the primary meaning of *sanctus* in Latin is not 'holy' or 'saintly' but 'inviolable', as befits its role as a principal part of *sancio*, 'to render inviolate'. (It is *sacer* which means 'holy' in that other sense.) What Montaigne tells us Homer did was not to wound some 'sainted' Venus (who might even unwittingly recall John Milton's wife) but to use his poetic licence to have Venus wounded in a war, despite that 'inviolability' to men's attacks which she in fact enjoyed (as Ennius had noted in early days when he called her 'sancta'). Since *sanctus* is also used by Cicero in this general sense it was well-known:

well-known too to students of the law (and what educated author in the Renaissance had not studied some law?) since Ulpian had defined *sanctum* in the *Digest* (1. 8. 9) as that which is 'ab iniuria hominum defensum'.

Legal Latin is much more commonly influential in Montaigne's French than may be often realised. When in the *Apologie de Raimond Sebond* we meet 'à quoy il n'ait interposé son decret' (II. 12. 439a), we are foxed or misled without a memory of *decretum interponere* ('to pronounce a decree'), an expression which (in some form or other) is found in many of the best authors including Cicero. Similarly the allusion in 'De l'experience' to jurisconsults who select 'mots solemnes' (III. 13. 1067b) is greatly weakened if taken to mean 'solemn' words and not 'formal' ones — 'customary formal expressions'. Montaigne is talking here about lawyers drawing up wills and testaments; he insists that when judged by lay minds these legal experts seek out obscure and opaque 'mots solemnes'. Such lawyers were doing their bounden duty! Papinian had warned that without such *sollennia*, wills were not valid. Montaigne is not condemning lawyers for using 'solemn' words but for being bound professionally to traditional jargon. And when writing of wills and lawyers he really did know what he was talking about.

Not infrequently his quasi-legal language is indebted to Cicero, directly or indirectly. So when he refers in 'De l'incommodité de la grandeur' to our difficulty in giving a 'jugement syncere', we might recall the use of *sincerus* in the sense of 'sound' or 'uncorrupt' in Cicero's *Orator* (VIII. 25): 'prudens sincerumque judicium' (cf. III. 7. 918b). And so on.

One hopes that at least *saincte* used for Venus would even now lead to hesitation and puzzlement. But what can a complete non-Latinist make unaided of the quip of 'ce philosophe ancien' cited in 'Sur des vers de Virgile' to explain why an old Greek philosopher could not get his hooks sexually into a young tyro: 'Mon amy, le hameçon ne mord pas à du fromage si frais' (III. 5. 894c). Hooking 'cheese' on a fishing-line makes one think vaguely of La Fontaine's 'Maître Corbeau, sur un arbre perché'. But *caseum* in classical Latin was a term of sexual admiration (not unlike 'cheesecake'), which would have helped readers to get the point of Diogenes Laertius' saying in his *Life of Bion*, duly latinised as:

41

'non enim, inquit, possibile est mollem caseum hamo attrahere' (cited *Edition municipale*, IV, p. 393, s.v., p. 140, line 8).

My own recent experience — and what has been told me by colleagues in France confirms it — is that Montaigne has become worryingly vague, opaque, and difficult for those who have no detailed idea of many of the shifts of meaning which have occurred since he wrote. In Montaigne (as indeed for analogous words in St Paul) *cœur* or *courage* often mean what we mean by 'mind' not 'heart'. We can therefore in ignorance be diverted into the area of emotions when the topic in fact concerns rationality. So when in 'De l'incommodité de la grandeur' Montaigne uses the expression 'J'esguise mon courage' (III. 7. 916b), he is doubtless rendering (correctly) *acuere mentem* ('to sharpen the mind') as in Cicero; when a little later he declares his dislike for having to 'fendre en adoration les presses' (917b) the notion behind 'en adoration' is impossible to recover unless one recalls that we are not being referred to 'adoration' in any modern sense but to that kissing and waving of the hand by which ancient deities or their statues were greeted: Montaigne, a gentleman, dislikes having to treat a crowd of courtiers as though they were pagan godlings.

Jokes can be weakened too, especially when they are on the coarse side. In Priapic contexts *tumor* means not only a commotion or a 'swelling' emotional state but, concretely, the swelling up of any part of the body including (with a smile) 'testium tumores et genitalium': which explains Zeno's otherwise obscure jest (by which he justified his starting away from some handsome youth who plonked down beside him): 'J'entends…que les medecins ordonnent le repos principalement, et deffendent l'emotion à toutes tumeurs' (III. 10. 1015c).

Similarly Montaigne's assertion that Venus — *not* Cupid by the way and certainly not that *amicitia* which he felt for his wife among other persons — is but 'le plaisir à descharger ses vases' (III. 5. 877c) comes with a trail of smiles when associated with those priapics in which *vasa* means not merely 'tool' or 'instrument' — 'vase' being far from its principal meaning — but more specifically penis or 'balls', a sense found ambiguously elsewhere (in Plautus for example). Venus is not 'emptying' or 'discharging' our 'vases' but 'unloading' or 'discharging' male genitalia as coarsely named among the Latins.

Of course (once aware of the vast reservoir of Latin meanings which feed the *Essais*) a judicious use of the Latin dictionaries can help a great deal. Difficulties arise when those we want to help cannot tell from the text itself that the meanings that we need to find are in fact to be sought from the Latin, since other or later meanings seem to make adequate sense. Dozens of such *faux amis* can be found, by no means all of them supplied with warning glosses in the texts available for study. One of them is 'importunité' (III. 8. 923b) in the sense of *importunitas* when applied to character ('unmannerliness', 'rudeness', etc.). Another is 'proprieté' as used in 'De la vanité' (III. 9. 985b) where Montaigne (despite what some glosses state) is not referring to 'clean' lodgings (those marked by 'propreté') but those marked by a 'certaine proprieté simple' that is, a certain kind of simplicity 'peculiar' to such country lodgings; a *proprietas* therefore. He likes 'rural simplicity'. Then there are those curious 'regles positives' (III. 5. 880c), an expression which in context is indeed puzzling unless 'positif' is given its Latin sense of 'imposed', as the antithesis to 'natural': the laws of our own invention, those of our parish-pump, are 'positives' ('arbitrary') and therefore the antithesis of 'celles de Dieu et du monde'.

The point at issue is a major one.

One usage which can leave the reader scratching his head in perplexity is Montaigne's statement that the pious among his Protestant enemies use the name of God neither as interjections nor exclamations (which is clear enough), 'ny pour tesmoignage, ny pour comparaison' (I. 56. 323a). It is important to understand what Montaigne means here, as he approves of his enemies' practice ('en quoy je trouve qu'ils ont raison'). These good, though mistaken, *réformés* refuse to use the name of God when giving testimony ('pour tesmoignage') or when swearing a contract ('pour comparaison'); one of the senses of *comparatio* in Latin being a contract or agreement.

Classical Allusions in Classical Contexts

Montaigne is so steeped in Latin culture that his associations of ideas are inevitably often those of the Latin authors who had formed his mind and the Latin language which had informed his studies. This fact can explain otherwise curious shifts of interest or, indeed, help to explain why a chapter has a title which does not lead directly on to what is talked about.

The clearest example of this is perhaps 'Des menteurs' (I. 9), a chapter more concerned at first, as we read it now, with a poor memory than with either fibbing or barefaced lying. I doubt if many of the reasonably literate readers of the day were at a loss to understand why. But our students might well be. It seems today almost playful and coy to start off a chapter on lying with the reflexion:

> Il n'est homme à qui il siese si mal de se mesler de parler de memoire.
>
> (I. 9. 34a)

But any lingering puzzlement would at once have been dispersed by the allusion, which in the *editio princeps* came very near the beginning (in the first half-a-dozen lines in fact) but eventually became pushed farther and farther away as some ten or more interpolations, some quite big, were brought into the text:

> Ce n'est pas sans raison qu'on dit que qui ne se sent point assez ferme de memoire, ne se doit pas mesler d'estre menteur. Je sçay bien que les grammairiens...
>
> (I. 9. 35a)

The source is Quintilian (IV. 2. 91-2), for whom the notion was already proverbial:

> Verumque est illud, quod vulgo dicitur, mendacem memorem esse oportere.

The proverb was so well-known that it was often cited (in its Latin form) in even quite popular Renaissance works.

What applies to whole chapters can also apply to detail, in the sense that glancing combinations of words may evoke specific texts or contexts. There can be a loss of comprehension and, indeed, a real aesthetic impoverishment, when glancing allusions to assumed common culture no longer achieve their end. When Montaigne alludes in his *Apologie de Raimond Sebond* to the 'stupid title' which Aristotle gave

44

to men, 'Dieux mortels' (II. 12. 489c), he is recalling not Aristotle's vast corpus of writings but a much more accessible remark of Cicero's in *De finibus bonorum et malorum* (II. 13. 40):

> Hi non viderunt, ut ad cursum equum, ad arandum bovem, ad indagandam canem, sic hominem ad duas res, ut ait Aristoteles, ad intellegendum et ad agendum esse natum, quasi mortalem deum...

In context it is not so much Aristotle as Cicero who thought too highly of Man. Which was one of the reasons why Montaigne (who rated Aristotle highly) did not think much of Cicero.

And what a shame it is if we do not pick up the glancing allusion to the 'Caucasia rupes' of Propertius (II. 1. 69) when we are told that all things 'branlent sans cesse: la terre, les rochers du Caucase...' (III. 2. 804b).

Classical Allusions in Contemporary Christian Contexts

This third category contains numerous examples but they are precisely the ones hardest for many readers to discover or to grasp. The very thorough work within the tradition which identifies Montaigne's classical sources in the void, beginning with Marie de Gournay and reaching its richest flowering with Pierre Villey, has had the inevitable result of leading to the supposition that Montaigne's culture was primarily classical and virtually confined to classical authors studied in the round. And of course there is some truth in that: he did know and love his Latin authors with a love and understanding rare at any time. But when he thrice cites Virgil on the nature of the soul (*Apologie de Raimond Sebond*, II. 12. 542), and when these three verses are also similarly cited to the same purpose in Melanchthon's *De anima* (and hence in a great many subsequent Renaissance works) we can be sure that Montaigne did not list them because he had independently recognised their relevance when enjoying Virgil in his book-room during a bout of poetry-reading. He had found them together in his reading of more modern books or in discussions with contemporaries.

When Montaigne is treating the philosophical attraction of death (which has, oddly, struck generations of readers as somehow anti-Christian or un-Christian) he is as close as possible to informed theological opinion within his Church in his day. A useful book which helped me to make this point when I first came across it in the fifties is one which I have alluded to in earlier studies but which many colleagues have told me cannot be found in many libraries. So I shall quote a sentence or two of it here, using the copy in the Bodleian at M.2.9.Th. (It is not cited as a source any more than Melanchthon was, but as a ruler against which can be judged both meaning and orthodoxy.)

Fray Bartholomaeus à Medina in his *Expositio in primam secundae Angelici doctoris* (Salamanca, 1588) discusses under *Quaestio V, articulus III* (f. 87 sq.) the question: 'Can anyone be blessed in this life?'

Bartholomaeus thus has to deal with the twin Thomist conclusions: 1) that man can indeed enjoy a *beatitudo imperfecta* this side of the grave; 2) that he cannot enjoy *perfecta beatitudo* this side of the grave.

Bartholomaeus points out that a major objection to these conclusions is that it would follow that all men would naturally desire to die ('Nam ex ea sequitur omnes homines naturali desiderio desiderare mortem'); 'but,' he adds, 'that is contrary to experience.' It is his refutation of the objections which can be raised to the second of these Thomist propositions which is of most interest to readers of two chapters of the *Essais* and which shows that Montaigne's texts and authorities were 'in the air' at the time:

Ad secundum argumentum confutandum, nonnulla sunt animadvertenda. In primis, omnes per appetitum sensitivum horremus mortem, ut malum terribile. Nam sensitiva pars, nil de felicitate alterius seculi iudicare potest; at per appetitum rationalem oportet ut appetamus mortem pro consecutione beatitudinis perfectae, quae in hac vita mortali haberi nequit. Quapropter multi philosophi pro consecutione huius felicitatis, quamvis de ea tenuissimam haberent cognitionem, sponte se morti tradiderunt.

Cicero in *prima Tuscul.* refert quendam Aegyptium Cyrenaeum prohibitum fuisse à Ptolomaeo Rege de incommodis huius vitae, & felicitate alterius disserere, quoniam his auditis multi sibi mortem consciscebant.

Ibidem commemorat alium, Ambrosiatem nomine, quem dicit cum nihil adversi sibi accidisset, se è muro in mare praecipitasse lecto

46

Platonis *lib. de immortalite animae*. Augu. Eugubinus *lib. 10 de perenni philosophia c. 10* refert alios philosophos, qui habebant in ore illam sententiam Domini, 'Qui odit animam suam in hoc mundo, in vitam aeternam custodit eam'.

Sed his praetermissis, quae incerta sunt, D. Paul. *ad Philip. 1* verissimè dicit; 'Cupio dissolvi, & esse cum Christo' et *ad Rom. 7* 'Infelix ego homo, quis me liberabit de morte corporis huius?'

[My italics and quotation marks. I have inserted Roman numbers in the translation to make identification easier.]

To refute the second argument [that it would follow that all men would naturally desire death] some remarks are necessary. Firstly we all are terrified of dying (it being a terrible evil), through our sensitive appetite. For the sensitive part can make no judgement about the happiness of the Next World; but through the rational appetite we ought to desire to die in order to obtain that perfect blessedness which cannot be had in this life. Which is why many philosophers, even though they had but the slenderest knowledge of it, have willingly killed themselves in order to obtain this happiness.

i) Cicero in *I Tusculan Disputations* alludes to a certain Cyrenaic of Egypt who was forbidden by King Ptolemy to lecture on the ills of this life and the happiness of the Next, because many, when they heard these things, sought their own deaths.

ii) In the same place, he [Cicero] recalls another philosopher named Ambrosiates who, he said, threw himself from a wall into the sea, despite his experiencing no misfortunes, after he had read Plato's dialogue 'On the Immortality of the Soul' [i.e. the *Phædo*]. Augustus Eugubinus in *De perenni philosophia*, Book 10, Chapter 10, refers to other philosophers who had on their lips Our Lord's saying, 'He that hateth his life [i.e. 'animam'] in this world shall keep it unto life eternal' [John 12. 25].

iii) But let us pass over such examples which lack certainty; St Paul in Philippians 1 [23] most truly said, 'I wish to be loosened asunder and to be with Christ', and in Romans 7 [24]: 'O wretched man that I am! Who will deliver me out of this body of death?'...

Bartholmaeus's two 'certain' examples — both from St Paul —

47

appear in their appropriate context in the *Essais*. To take the last one first: Philippians 1. 23 was so central a text that it was virtually always cited in an abbreviated Latin form, as it is by Bartholomaeus here: 'Cupio dissolvi' and so on. That is the Latin text which lies behind one of the versions of Montaigne:

> Je veuil estre dissout, dirions nous, et estre aveques Jesus-Christ.

And Montaigne goes on, like Bartholomaeus and others, to link this text of Paul with Platonising suicides:

> La force du discours de Platon, de l'immortalité de l'ame, poussa bien aucuns de ses disciples à la mort, pour joïr plus promptement des esperances qu'il leur donnoit.
>
> (II. 12. 445a)

On the other hand the earlier use of Philippians 1. 23 by Montaigne, also in the context of suicide, in 'Coustume de l'isle de Cea' (II. 3), more closely follows the actual words of the Vulgate, which reads:

> desiderium habens dissolvi, et esse cum Christo, multo magis melius.

With that compare 'Coustume de l'isle de Cea' (II. 3. 360a):

> Mais on desire aussi quelque fois la mort pour l'esperance d'un plus grand bien [= 'multo magis melius']. Je desire...estre dissoult [= 'desiderium habens dissolvi'] pour estre avec Jesus-Christ.

The remainder of the sentence links together other texts cited by Bartholomaeus. First comes St Paul again:

> et: Qui me desprendra de ces liens?

Which is a not very literal rendering of Romans 7. 24:

> Quis me liberabit de corpore mortis hujus?

The looseness of the rendering may be attributed either to an intermediate source used by Montaigne, or to a desire to avoid a 'Protestant' air of textual word-chopping or (instead or as well) to a memory of the fact that the word 'bonds' (*liens*; Latin *catenae* and above all *vincula*) are leitmotivs of St Paul. At all events this is again linked with ii) in the translation of Bartholomaeus:

> Cleombrotus Ambraciota, ayant leu le Phædon de Platon, entra en si grand appetit de la vie advenir que, sans autre occasion, il s'alla precipiter en la mer.
>
> (II. 3. 360a)

In both Montaigne and Bartholomaeus we are dealing with an 'appetit', an *appetitus*. And in both cases, as the contexts make clear, it is the *appetitus rationalis* — the appetite which, when not corrected, makes suicide so attractive to the better sort of Platonic philosopher.

The third example relevant to Montaigne (no. i in the translation) does not fully appear in the *Essais* until the marginalia were written in the Bordeaux copy. It concerns 'De la diversion' (III. 4. 833):

> [B] Les disciples de Hegesias, qui se font mourir de faim, eschauffez des beaux discours de ses leçons, [C] et si dru que le Roy Ptolomée luy fit defendre d'entretenir plus son escole de ces homicides discours, [B] ceux là ne considerent point la mort en soy [i.e. the act of dying], ils ne la jugent point: ce n'est pas là où ils arrestent leur pensée; ils courent, ils visent à un estre nouveau.

That is what Bartholomaeus also means in i) above. His 'Cyrenaic' is indeed Hegesias of Cyrene, a philosopher of the time of Ptolemy Soter who was driven out of Alexandria because of the dire effects of his teachings.

That authors as different as Montaigne — a French provincial Catholic layman — and Fray Bartholomaeus à Medina — a scholarly lamp of the Order of Preachers working in Salamanca — should both use the same proof-texts and examples shows that those texts constituted important theological commonplaces in the 1580s (and 1590s) and are knowledgeably and powerfully used as such by Montaigne.

CLASSICAL NOTIONS IN THEIR CONTEXT

Classical Allusions in Contemporary Political Contexts

Here I have only one example to cite since this field has not, I think, been much worked. It is, I suggest, a revealing example. It throws a flood of light on to an important corner of Montaigne's religio-political attitudes.

The final words which bring their uneasy conclusion to 'De la liberté de conscience' (II. 19) are arresting and, to those who do not have any idea where they come from, actively misleading. Montaigne was evidently ill at ease with the official tolerance of religious dissent which was being forced upon the Most Christian King. This chapter is doubtless connected with the *Paix de Monsieur* and the Edict of Beaulieu (May 1576). Montaigne's reflexions and reservations can be interestingly compared and contrasted with a treatise printed in 1586 by his own original publisher: M. Bertin's *Traicté de la liberté de la conscience* (Simon Millanges, Bordeaux).

The enforced recognition of a limited 'freedom of conscience' was disliked by Montaigne both because it was indeed imposed upon an unwilling monarch and because he suspected that it would foment divisions (which in the past had been the intention of the Emperor Julian the Apostate in pursuing similar policies) and would therefore weaken or destroy Christianity. For Montaigne it was a policy which did little honour to the piety ('devotion') of the French monarchy which bowed to it, except in so far as it was a concession wrenched from it:

> Et si croy mieux, pour l'honneur de la devotion de nos rois, c'est que, n'ayans peu ce qu'ils vouloient, ils ont fait semblant de vouloir ce qu'ils pouvoient.
>
> (II. 19. 672a)

To grasp the meaning and to feel the impact of these words at this climax, we must see them for what they are: an echo of a quip in Montaigne's favourite comic author, Terence. It occurs in the *Andria*:

> quaeso edepol, Charine, quoniam non potest, id fieri quod vis,
> id velis quod possit.
>
> (III. 1. 5)

50

(Pon my word, Charinus, since what you wish is impossible,
Wish what *is* possible.)

Montaigne is in other words making a wry statement with a twisted
smile. That itself tells us much. But he was not the first to do this
with the aid of Terence. In 1546 there appeared a little booklet (8⁰,
eight leaves signed [A1, 2] iii, iv, y, — A5 thus mis-signed) entitled:

PASQVIL-/LVS NOVVS TEREN/TIANUS, QVI SINE FELLE/
nigro circum   praecordia ludit. / PASQVILLUS/ALIVS
CALENDIS DECEMB./ANNO M. D. XLV.   RO-/MAE
ADFIXVS. /*Anno* M. D. XLVI. / [no place]

It in fact, as the title shows, contains two short works, the first a list of
quotations from Terence applied to various persons and events; the
second some pasquinades which had been affixed in Rome (to the statue
of Pasquino no doubt, that is to the so-called statue of Hercules) in
December 1545.

The applications of the words or phrases are really very apt and
amusing. The one that concerns us here appears at Aiii^r under the
heading:

Rex Franciae ad pacem compulsus

Quoniam id fieri quod uis non potest, velis id quod possit

(The King of France, compelled to make peace

Since what you wish is impossible, wish what is *possible*).

So a quip which was going the rounds since 1545 or 1546 and
probably at least since the Peace of Crépy (1544) is reapplied to the
events of some thirty years later. Such *bons mots* normally circulate by
word of mouth and may leave few traces, even nowadays. The fortunate
survival of this booklet of pasquinades enables us to understand a jest
which a man like Montaigne would doubtless have made with the

expectation that his reasonably well-informed humanist reader would savour its wry humour.

It also helps to explain something which long puzzled me: why Montaigne in the context of what seems to be the granting of freedom of conscience resulting from one specific edict of Henri III should have referred to the honour and piety of 'nos rois' in the plural. We can assume that Terence's quip after being applied to François Ier, then stood a turn for Henri II and for François II under pressure from Coligny's demands for freedom of worship, and finally for Henri III.

5

Montaigne and the Exercise of Paradox:
Essais III. 12

John O'Brien

Twentieth-century readers, if they retain any interest at all in the study of the physiognomy, do so primarily in virtue of the pioneering work contained in Lavater's *Physiognomische Fragmente* of 1775-8. Even Lavater is hardly well-known these days, compared with Balzac's perhaps more famous fascination with the same phenomenon. The Renaissance, by contrast, knew that the topic had long historical antecedents and it was acquainted with a range of classical writing about the physiognomy, notably pseudo-Aristotle, Adamantius, and Polemon.[1] Alongside editions and translations of these and other classical physiognomers, there were independent studies too, starting back in the fifteenth century with printings of Petrus de Abano's *Liber compilationis phisionomie* and Michael Scott's *De procreatione et hominis phisionomia*.[2] Moreover the genre not only has an impressive classical pedigree, it also has equally impressive classical practitioners. Foremost among these, as Giovanni Battista della Porta points out in his *De humana physiognomonia* of 1586, is Socrates. Socrates uses the physiognomy as a sure index of character; it has accurate cognitive results and, della Porta adds, is likewise the key to self-knowledge.[3]

It is a *doxa* such as this which lies behind the very palpable worry voiced by Montaigne at a crucial moment far advanced in 'De la phisionomie'. He has just been recommending Socrates' attitude to death, which like all else in the Greek philosopher testifies to his 'nayfveté et...simplicité' (III. 12. 1037b) and he is about to open the final section of the essay in which he recounts two anecdotes about the strange fits of fortune to which possession of a face can lead. Between these two segments are placed the following remarks:

> [B] Socrates, qui a esté un exemplaire parfaict en toutes grandes qualitez, j'ay despit qu'il eust rencontré un corps et un visage si vilain, comme ils disent, et disconvenable à la beauté de son ame, [C] luy si amoureux et si affolé de la beauté. Nature luy fit injustice. [B] Il n'est rien plus vraysemblable que la conformité et relation du corps à l'esprit.
>
> (III. 12. 1057)

In 1588, the essay continued as follows:

> Il n'est pas à croire que cette dissonance aduienne sans quelque accident, qui a interrompu le cours ordinaire: come il disoit de sa laideur qu'elle en accusoit iustement autant en son ame, s'il ne l'eust corrigée par institution.[4]

By 1595, this last sentence is split in half at 'come', the first half is suppressed and replaced by a quotation from Cicero's *Tusculan Disputations* and an *alongeail* returning to the vexed business of the countenance and character correspondence.

Montaigne is citing here a familiar argument about the relation between physiognomy and temperament; the relation was commonly thought to be an intrinsic one, a relation of cause and effect. Corporeal beauty is the signifier which has its signified in spiritual beauty. The bonding between the two elements of the sign is not in question, nor the motivation of the sign which this implies. This is an argument for which Montaigne feels considerable sympathy: 'Il n'est rien plus vraysemblable que la conformité et relation du corps à l'esprit' and he retained this comment even after the alterations made to this passage after 1588. However, Montaigne is then faced with a problem, for Socrates is the counter-example to this law of general probability: he illustrates the disjunction between *corps* and *esprit*. Socrates, the 'exemplaire parfaict en toutes grandes qualitez', is suddenly out of phase with the state of nature. He constitutes a contradiction where, as 'exemplaire parfaict', no contradiction should exist.

In 1588, Montaigne explains this by saying that some accident has interrupted the usual course of things, a remark which highlights the accepted naturalism of the sign. He then substantiates his supposition by reference to an anecdote well-known to writers of physiognomical treatises: Socrates' meeting with the physiognomer Zopyrus,[5] recounted by Cicero in *Tusculan Disputations* IV. 37 and again in *De fato* V. 10. It is an anecdote sufficiently popular to act as a reference point for Renaissance writers on the physiognomy.[6] Cicero's two versions of the story contain some important differences which it will be necessary to highlight. The shorter of the two accounts is in *Tusculan Disputations*, where Cicero is making the anti-deterministic point that anger and melancholy are evils constituted for the health of the soul and are curable ('sanabiles'). Socrates is the selected instance. Zopyrus reads 'multa...vitia' in his features, for which he is derided by Socrates' followers, but baled out ('sublevatus') by Socrates himself who admits his failings but says he has expelled them by reason ('illa sibi insita, sed ratione a se deiecta diceret'). In *De fato*, Zopyrus calls Socrates 'stupidum...et bardum' and 'etiam mulierosum', a remark which draws a laugh from Alcibiades. Socrates is credited with no reply, but Cicero himself comments that Socrates' extirpation of these vices cannot be due to natural causes, but rather to 'voluntate, studio, disciplina'.

Clearly, Montaigne's 1588 version is close to *Tusculan Disputations* — Socrates admits that his ugliness 'en accusoit justement autant en son ame, s'il ne l'eust corrigée par institution' (III. 12. 1058b) — except for the detail 'par institution', which looks like a free equivalent of 'studium' and 'disciplina' from *De fato*. 'Institution', 'training', seems specifically to imply philosophical training. This is a point made independently in two places, first by Alexander of Aphrodisias when he attributes Socrates' moral rehabilitation to φιλοσοφίας ἄσκησις,[7] and second — in the French Renaissance itself — by Antoine du Moulin who gives his own version of the *Tusculan Disputations* story, ending with Socrates saying that he would have turned out corrupt, had he not offered himself to correction by philosophy ('asseruit se talem omnino evasurum fuisse, nisi se philosophiae corrigendum exhibuisset').[8] The importance of training in the formation of human character is likewise underscored by Erasmus, as when he exclaims, 'at homines, mihi crede, non nascuntur, sed finguntur',[9] or above all, when he establishes the Plutarchan-inspired maxim which Margolin considers the keynote of the whole of *De pueris instituendis*: 'efficax res est natura, sed hanc vincit efficacior institutio'.[10] Equally revealingly, Erasmus later cites pseudo-Aristotle on the physiognomy to speak of natural signs of human nature before going on to show what can be achieved through training.[11] Hence Socrates' interpretation of his own behaviour in Montaigne has impeccable analogues in Erasmian educational theory as an example of the triumph of art over nature. One might note, furthermore, that in aligning himself with Socrates' own explanation of his moral redressment, Montaigne is also, if no doubt distantly, reacting against the patristic view of Socrates, evident in John Cassian, Eusebius, and Origen, which varies between outright condemnation and qualified approval.[12] Already, then, Montaigne's championing of Socrates as 'exemplaire parfaict' involves subtextual choices and preferences.

One solution to the discrepancy of countenance and its significance is therefore to admit the discrepancy but to seek accredited ways of overcoming the obstacle by recourse to a version of moral perfectibility. The advantage of this position, as André Tournon observes, is that 'institution' is no longer an extraneous accretion remedying Socrates' deficiencies of character, but the realisation of his authentic human nature.[13] In effect, Montaigne's argument up to this point works by marshalling authority and counter-authority; it proceeds by arguing for and against certain types of reading. Montaigne directs the reader's attention to the authoritative *loci* as a preparation for shifting the thrust of the reader's understanding away from the *doxa* which represents the standard contemporary reading, while nonetheless allowing for the force and persuasiveness of that *doxa*. What emerges from this activity is that the dichotomy between countenance and what it predicates is not wholly a natural sign: it is a natural sign in part created from simple empirical observation, but in part also the product of a conventional reading — a *doxa* which conceals its cultural origins under the guise of a natural sign. Complicit with the conduct of Montaigne's argument at this juncture, the citing of authoritative *loci* is never directly acknowledged, is never raised beyond the level of the most discreet allusion; and by 1595, the reader is left to calculate the range of allusive response he is required to supply — first the brief indication of an established *doxa*; finally a story drawn from *Tusculan Disputations*; between them, from elsewhere in the same work, an overt quotation which accentuates rather than relaxes the congruity of body and soul.

A further possible interpretation is now intimated by Montaigne, and it offers an alternative solution to the dissociation of signifier and signified in Socrates. This solution leaves the problem in one sense unresolved by locating in it a permanent yet permissible disjunction labelled 'paradox'. To an important degree, this solution is prepared by establishing the reading inspired by *doxa* in order the more effectively to move against the *doxa* (παρὰ τὴν δόξαν). This second form of recovering the problem, while it is never openly named as paradox by Montaigne and is indeed less observed or perceived than created, has in turn its own *locus classicus*, a *locus*, moreover, signalled at the outset of 'De la phisionomie' as the generator of strategic dichotomies between appearance and reality. This new reading features, one hardly needs to say, the Silenic Socrates, a figure familiar to Montaigne from Ficino's Latin translation of the *Symposium* (a copy of which he owned), yet also mediated to him particularly through Erasmus' adage 'Sileni Alcibiadis'.[14] In an analogous context, and with equally obvious reference to the figure of Socrates, Erasmus himself speaks in *De pueris instituendis* of the bestial exterior of man being refined through the process of education.[15] Nor is Erasmus the sole instance. Elsewhere within the Renaissance, the figure of Socrates as living paradox also occurs in Ortensio Lando's *Paradossi* (famously adapted into French by Charles Estienne), where Socrates is the prime instance selected to illustrate the theme, 'il vault mieulx estre laid, que beau'.[16]

Historical precedents for the use of paradox covered a range of possibilities, which, as the analyses of Alain Michel have made clear, were themselves not all of the same type or function.[17] In the early thinker, Heraclitus, paradox represented a contradiction in human experience, as in his famous dictum 'one cannot set foot in the same river twice'. Stoic paradoxes — familiar to Renaissance audiences through Cicero's *Paradoxa Stoicorum* — overturned everyday language by paradox in the service of rationalism; hence propositions of the type 'only the sage is free, even when he is a slave'. In Platonic thought, paradox constituted a criticism of appearance (*doxa*) in the interests of transcendental principles. Socrates in particular expounded philosophy through paradox and by fixing on Socrates as source of paradox as well as by quoting and questioning *doxa*, Montaigne is following a recognisable classical paradigm. Truth in the Platonic view can only be reached by disposing of the *doxa*, and in this strong sense paradox will be the instrument which serves the logical elaboration of a dialectical scheme designed for this purpose. It is, one recalls, paradox as scheme which helps organise the opening pages of 'De la phisionomie' which deals with the deceptiveness of appearances and the difficulty of perceiving anything but appearances.

A second, equally familiar and related version of paradox is the reversing proposition: an individual proposition, or a series of individual propositions, frequently entailing problems of verification. This type of paradox can overlap with the previous variety. Lando's *Paradossi* fall into this category in that, as 'propos contre la commune opinion', they are designed to challenge appearances, yet their reversals are to be tested and verified. Such reversals of accepted opinions are, writes Donne in his letter accompanying the publication of *Paradoxes and Problems*, the reason why paradoxes are 'nothings':[18] once resolved, they vanish. Culler neatly summarises their working: 'The correct interpretation of the contradictory terms is presumed to be that which makes the paradox acceptable and the process of understanding is a search for meanings which would make it so.'[19] Montaigne's paradox is not of this type, since his implied proposition is not of the order 'ugliness is beauty', nor will verification necessarily entail annulation of the paradox. His is not, in that case, an individual proposition about Socrates, but already part of a larger argument which Socrates illustrates and is in turn illustrated by. The paradox here centres therefore on the question of representation and is not so much a linguistic problem as a figural problem. It is not the content of the paradoxical proposition which is in question, but the configuration itself, the *coincidentia oppositorum*. Like all paradoxes, this paradox names the place of a disjunction. The disjunction, when formalised, now has the status of a figure within rhetoric; the figure helps to resolve a contradiction within nature by holding out the promise that it will, in Fontanier's words, 'frappe[r] l'intelligence par le plus étonnant accord, et produi[re] le sens le plus vrai, comme le plus profond et le plus énergique'.[20] This resolution to a paradox has clear affinities with the movement from appearance (the contradiction between the constitutive elements) to reality (the resolving of the contradiction by the establishment of truth). As a consequence, the paradox denotes not just a name for a disjunction but a use for disjunction, a means of mobilising it, of shaking it free from its stasis. To anticipate a little, Montaigne will be calling attention to, and examining, this way of conceiving of the resolution of a paradox of figural representation.

In the post-1588 additions to this part of the essay, Montaigne returns to the problem and offers new solutions: Socrates must be speaking ironically when he talks of correcting his soul, for 'jamais ame si excellente ne se fit elle mesme' (1058c). Or again — and this is the approach which is developed at some length — ugliness is some superficial deformity which is 'de moindre prejudice à l'estat de l'esprit et a peu de certitude en l'opinion des hommes' (1057c). In a further extension to Montaigne's thought, a new element is introduced to disprove the universal validity of the correlation between countenance and character: an appeal to experience, which shows that the countenance is 'une foible garantie' (1059b) and fair looks do not betoken a fair nature. This case is felt with particular acuity by Montaigne, since La Boétie was in the same category as Socrates, moral beauty concealed within physical ugliness. All these are ways of crediting the paradox and demonstrating that the conventional reading of a natural phenomenon has given rise to a causal ordering in which moral beauty and goodness and physical beauty are taken to be innately coupled together. Having once disestablished the necessity of this causality, Montaigne then remotivates each component independently, face and character in separate sequence. Nevertheless, the possibility of such an explanation does not go unqualified. Despite his willingness to credit the real force of these exceptions, Montaigne registers his distance from the terms of the paradox. His reactions are already in place by 1588 and in the years following, he does not modify them:

J'ay pris, comme j'ay dict ailleurs, bien simplement et cruement pour mon regard ce precepte ancien: que nous ne sçaurions faillir à suivre nature, que le souverain precepte c'est de se conformer à elle. Je n'ay pas corrigé, comme Socrates, par force de la raison mes complexions naturelles, et n'ay aucunement troublé par art mon inclination.

(1059b)

A later *alongeail* refers to 'cette raison, qui redresse Socrates de son vicieux ply' (1059c), and in both readings Montaigne is amplifying Socrates' own comment recorded in *Tusculan Disputations*. Socrates is now the exponent and beneficiary of *recta ratio*. In 1588, the earlier version of the phrase 'par force de la raison' read 'par institution & force...',[21] an expression which reinforces the echoes established earlier and makes it sympathetic to Erasmian *loci* such as that which notes that Providence has endowed man with reason, but has left the greatest part to *institutio*.[22] If this comparison is justified, it confirms André Tournon's observation that the 1586 version of the essay is a sustained meditation on the connection between nature and 'institution' as they occur in the person of Socrates: this is now further strengthened by Erasmian reference.[23]

By a further twist in the argument, the difficulties in deploying Socrates now become apparent, and they are difficulties which arise from the very project of training nature through art. This particular antinomy is a long-established one, but it now affects the two new signifiers introduced in the course of the discussion, Socrates and Montaigne. Socrates stands for the overlaying of nature by art; Montaigne stands for nature without that overlay. This development is the more perturbing because shortly before, Socrates' 'parler et vivre' had been characterised as 'l'extreme degré de perfection et de difficulté: l'art n'y peut joindre' (1055b). But by previously disallowing the link between face and character to be operative in Socrates' case, Montaigne has altered the relationship of Socrates to nature, for paradox's relation to its establishing ground is that of contradiction. Once this disestablishment is implemented, it can no longer be taken for granted that the natural-ness of Socrates is grounded in nature. The grounding for the two elements, instead of residing outside the figure, now resides in the contradictory unity of the figure itself. Culler's comments on a related topic point to the problem at issue here: 'Paradox...calls attention to itself as language and stimulates, as a corollary of the interpretative process that the form requires, a reflection on the deceptive power of language.'[24] The endorsing of paradox through the image of the Silenic Socrates raises the issue of whether paradox as an art-form does not transform contingent relations in nature and experience into necessary relations in language. Since the language of paradox assimilates and shapes in virtue of its own shapeliness, it by the same token reifies this contingency. If paradox can be shown to exist in nature, then no difficulty arises, because the link is motivated: the figure of paradox will simply represent a natural phenomenon. However, if paradox does not exist in nature, only a contingent juxtaposition of ugliness and beauty, then there is nothing to ground the figure of paradox. Paradox itself, on this account, discloses a broader paradox. On the one hand — and this is the clear implication of Montaigne's own comment — nature and art stand apart in such a way that art represents a deviation from nature. On the other hand, art has a privileged relationship with nature such that it accounts for one of the essential mechanisms of nature, its juxtaposition of opposites. Paradox as a figure, it appears, is from one direction in close liaison with nature, while from another in separation from it.

A related consideration also arises. While nature relies on language to represent it, nonetheless language tends to represent a disjunction in nature as an antithesis, a figure which should be distinguished from anacoluthon or discontinuity. Typically, a paradox conceived in terms of its figural properties will constitute both an antithesis and an expected harmony, in that its construction denies, but its result allows, a desired negotiation between incompatibles: in Socrates' case ugliness and beauty. The paradox will accordingly move through the discord of surface contradiction to the underlying harmony of resolution: antithesis yields to synthesis in view of the preference for affinity which, evidenced by the predominance of tropes of ressemblance, remains the prior assumption as well as the presumed conclusion of a rhetorical naming. And Fontanier's definition of paradox (to take one standard example) fosters this belief by associating intelligibility with harmony and depth of meaning. Since questions of affinity are central to the portrayal of Socrates, what is affected primarily by this process is Socrates' status as exemplar, specifically named as such in the phrase 'exemplaire parfaict en toutes grandes qualitez'. The very concept of Socrates as *exemplaire*, as model, introduces the idea of affinity, an affinity between two lives, one prior to the other, reflecting in that way the larger fact that representation supposes a prior representable which is duly represented. In the early stages of 'De la phisionomie', Socrates' 'mouvement naturel et commun' (1037b) is presented for the reader's sympathy and potential imitation. The thrust of the reader's expectation, working alongside the incremental logic of the narrative, is therefore, naturally enough, that some acclimitisation of Socrates as paradox will be made each time that Montaigne takes up his own relation to the model. However the essay reverses that expectation; it runs against our horizon of expectation, just as it runs against *doxa*. The representation of Socrates at this point in the essay consequently stands as a paradox within a paradox since Montaigne's discomfort with this representation travels purposely against the grain of this text which sets out precisely to demonstrate that Socrates' 'mouvement naturel et commun' is greater, more inherently worthy of admiration and imitation, than standard *exempla*: Socrates dethrones Caesar, 'la nayfveté et la simplicité' supplant heroic biography.

Such unpredictability is, of course, accountable as an *a priori* feature of the technique of paradox as such (Quintilian, for instance, calls it 'surprise', 'inopinatum', in recognition of just this quality),[25] but it also throws into relief the nature of the figure, the fact that paradox relies not on an affinity but on a disjunction, a demonstrable lack of affinity. The paradox acclimatises but, as with the cannibals of Montaigne's essay, also retains a measure of alterity. The alterity of paradox is presented in the figure of Socrates; and to use Socrates as *exemplaire* is to use Socrates as *exemplaire* of paradox, it is to carry through the consequences of Socrates as 'le paradoxe fait homme, ou l'homme, dans son essence paradoxale', as Margolin describes him.[26] And for the force of that alterity to be fully effective, it is conveyed by allowing the contradiction to subsist between adoption of Socrates as model and the modification of that model. If figural discourse is open to the objection that it enforces a form of closure, then Montaigne dramatises here the position at which the duality of imitator and imitated never fully closes or resolves into formal symmetry. The paradox will not resolve back into benign balance or synthesis, because it is not a propositional paradox but a paradox of figural representation.[27]

In one sense, the essay confirms the experimental criteria used, after 1588, to disqualify the outright accreditation of character from facial features. In another sense, the upshot of the piece lies elsewhere. For if the paradox is simply exhausted by verification because falsified by experience, then its fate is to revert to being a nothing, in Donne's description, and it threatens to controvert the model by radical curtailment of Socrates' potential as an exegetical force. Yet it is an uncomfortable fact that Montaigne can register his difference from the model here, but continue elsewhere to treat him as exemplary. In fact, these alternatives still limit the range of the paradox. The 'either...or...' view supposes that the paradox is either an affinity or its opposite. What this paradox reveals is neither an affinity nor its opposite. The verification of the model does not automatically entail dismissal of the model, because the paradox suspends the straightforward implementation of alternatives, and that suspension is marked by highlighting the point at which affinities between imitator and imitated turn, when reinscribed, and become differences and distinctions. To do otherwise would be to diminish the potency of the differences which paradox embodies.

In retrospect, two different versions of Socrates could be said to be presented in 'De la phisionomie' and they arise from the imbrication of two different varieties of paradox. In so far as Socrates is deployed to unhinge and fissure common misconceptions, he can be seen as the exemplary tool by which paradox breaks through the *doxa* of appearances. To that extent, he acts on the diegesis as if from without. This first way of employing Socrates — as though he were purely instrumental — is plainly metalinguistic, but there is no reason to be suspicious of it provided that the instrument displays properties distinct from and uncontaminated by the first-order properties upon which it is commenting. As long as Socrates is used to illustrate the paradox he himself embodies, there is no necessary contradiction: the disjunction between a form and a character can readily be assimilated to the abstract disjunction between appearance and reality. To adopt paradox as *exemplaire* might itself sound a logical impossibility, yet it remains a feasible project provided that within the model the affinities outweigh the discrepancies. The point at which the paradox changes character is that at which the affinities are no longer perceptible, with the result that the paradoxicality of the paradox reasserts itself. It is when Socrates as sign is placed in relation to further signs — art and nature — that difficulties arise. In the light of this addition to the enquiry, it now happens that the first type of paradox, in which Socrates acted as solution, is part of an argument within a second paradox and cannot be kept clear of it. In so far, then, as he is himself embroiled in paradox, his ideality as model is placed inside rather than outside the terms of the analysis; he is acted upon by paradox. In view of paradox's notorious propensity for regress into deeper paradox, it might, of course, prove possible to construct additional figural paradoxes to sublate these first two, but they would always be subordinate to the fact that their figurative force would fall inside rather than outside the discursive field and could not be taken as covering the whole of that field without themselves becoming enmeshed in paradox. The figure of paradox is, in other words, eccentric to its own construction and it is that eccentricity, implying the non-closure of the figure, that Montaigne foregrounds here.

In the broadest terms, then, Montaigne is commenting on the conflictual crossing of mimesis, or representation of Socrates, with diegesis, or the narrative universe in which representations occur. In its desire to constitute for the reader a natural image of Socrates, 'De la phisionomie' passes from voice to face, first quoting Socrates' apologia directly and at length (1052-4). But no such unimpeded access is possible when the essay moves on to the philosopher's face. The project falters, and the face becomes instead a worrying crux, producing ever-increasing explanations for its failure to conform, explanations which themselves draw on borrowed voices — reported narrative by or about Socrates, allusions alternating with quotation. The face is the sign of a breaking of form, of which paradox, that oxymoron of conjunctive disjunction, is the realisation. Once broken form is reached, the essayist cannot go back, and he does not. When the narrative is resumed, he postpones his portrait at least for the length of this essay and transfers to his own face. Yet this is not tantamount to claiming that he reverts simply to the original *doxa*-reading. Montaigne now incorporates into his account of his two adventures a primary feature occurring in his discussion of Socrates' character; and that is the notion of 'accident' by which Nature, unjustly, has endowed Socrates with 'un corps et un visage si vilain'. In taking further the question of the physiognomy as sign, Montaigne allows for the part played by fortune in endowing him with honest looks, and he embraces his fortune: 'suis homme en outre qui me commets volontiers à la fortune et me laisse aller à corps perdu entre ses bras' (1060-1061b). By the same token, fortune also plays a role in the providential interpretation of that sign:

note how Montaigne's release from the brigands is due to 'une soudaine et tres-inopinée mutation qui leur print' (1062b), an idea he repeats shortly afterwards: 'La vraye cause d'un changement si nouveau et de ce ravisement, sans aucune impulsion apparente...certes je ne sçay pas bien encores quelle elle est' (*ibidem*). Montaigne thereby escapes death as Socrates could not. He does not need a voice to urge away a sentence of death: his honest looks 'speak' naturally for him. Disaster falls instead on those very captors who spare his life; but they do not all share the same fortune as Montaigne, or as each other: one is still alive to tell the tale, the other not long since killed. 'C'est une foible garantie que la mine' (1059b): it could be the motto of this essay which richly complicates the possibilities of connection between models for self-knowledge and actual self-knowledge, fortune and form, living and its representation. For a piece which immediately precedes 'De l'experience', that seems only fitting.

NOTES

1 A full account of the manuscript and printed traditions is given in Richard Förster's Teubner edition, *Scriptores physiognomonici Graeci et Latini*, 2 vols (Leipzig, 1893), I, prolegomena. Pseudo-Aristotle was printed as early as 1472, with the *editio princeps* of Adamantius following on in 1540 (French translation by J. Lebon: Paris, 1556), and that of Polemon in 1545. Förster is still the standard modern edition of these authors.

2 Petrus de Abano: *editio princeps*, Padua, 1474. The work was written in 1295: see Förster, I. clxx; Michael Scott: *editio princeps*, Venice, 1477.

3 G. B. della Porta, *De humana physiognomonia* (Naples, 1602), sig. A3^{r-v} and p. 9. The first edition of this work dates from 1586.

4 *Les Essais de Michel de Montaigne*, publiés d'après l'exemplaire de Bordeaux, par Fortunat Strowski et François Gebelin (5 vols, 1906-23), III (Bordeaux, 1919), pp. 351-2.

5 For further information on Zopyrus, see Pauly-Wissowa, *Realencyclo-pädie des classischen Altertumswissenschaft*, second series, vol. X A (Munich, 1972), art. 'Zopyros', entry (3), cols 768-9. The incident is also related and investigated by Förster, I. vii-xiii. The background to the classical physiognomical tradition is provided in

Pauly-Wissowa, vol. XX. 1 (Stuttgart, 1941), art. 'Physiognomik', cols 1064-74.

6 For two such instances, see Petrus de Abano, *Liber compilationis phisionomie* (Padua, 1474), f. 2^V (*Tusculan Disputations* version); and della Porta, *De humana physiognomonia*, ed. cit., sig. $A3^V$ (*Tusculan Disputations* version) and p. 117 (*De fato* version).

7 Alexander of Aphrodisias, *On Fate*, edited by R. W. Sharples (London, 1983), p. 183 (= *De fato*, VI (171. 18)). Sharples's commentary gives further references for the probable origin of the story, concluding: 'It seems likely that the story was originally simply a protreptic to philosophy and that its connection with the issue of determinism was secondary' (p. 130). A number of editions of Alexander's work were printed during the Renaissance: see further F. Edward Cranz, 'Alexander Aphrodisiensis', in *Catalogus Translationum et Commentariorum: Mediaeval and Renaissance Latin Translations and Commentaries. Annotated Lists and Guides*, I (Washington, 1960), pp. 107-11.

8 Antoine du Moulin, *De diversa hominum natura* (Lyons, 1549), p. 6.

9 Erasmus, *Declamatio de pueris statim ac liberaliter instituendis*, edited by Jean-Claude Margolin, THR, 77 (Geneva, 1966), p. 389, 493b. Interestingly enough, Villey glosses 'institution' (p. 1058, n. 2). For the part played by Erasmus' treatise in Montaigne's own education, see Roger Trinquet, *La Jeunesse de Montaigne* (Paris, 1972), pp. 251-304 and 305-40.

10 Erasmus, ed. cit., p. 385, 492a and p. 487, n. 96 for Margolin's comments.

11 Erasmus, ed. cit., p. 411, 499e-f.

12 John Cassian, *Collationes patrum* XIII. 5. 3, is the fiercest critic, supplying Socrates' reply in which the philosopher admits his pederasty. Eusebius, *Praeparatio evangelica* VI. 9. 22 quotes extensively from Alexander of Aphrodisias, *De fato* VI, in the context of emphasising the possibility for improving human nature. Origen, *Contra Celsum* I. 33, mentions Zopyrus along with Loxias and Polemon.

13 André Tournon, *Montaigne: la glose et l'essai* (Lyons, 1983), pp. 276-7.

14 Erasmus, *Adagia* III. 3. 1. For recent work on this aspect of Montaigne's essay, see Raymond B. Waddington, 'Socrates in Montaigne's "Traicté de la phisionomie"', *Modern Language Quarterly*, XLI (1980), 328-45. Waddington refers in the course of

his article to Floyd Gray, 'Montaigne and the *Memorabilia*', *Studies in Philology*, LVIII (1961), 130-9, and Elaine Limbrick, 'Montaigne and Socrates', *Renaissance and Reformation*, IX (1972-3), 46-57.

15 Ed. cit., pp. 391-3, 493d-494a.

16 Ortensio Lando, *Paradoxes, ce sont propos contre la commune opinion* (Paris, 1553), pp. 22-7. The general proposition in paradox 2 is this: 'Et s'il fault rapporter & apparier la beaulté de l'esprit a celle du corps: ne trouuez vous pas plus grand nombre de gens difformes auoir esté saiges & ingenieux, que de beaulx & bien formez personnaiges?' (p. 22). Socrates is cited along with Aesop as the clearest illustration of this idea. Estienne's adaptation omits paradoxes 11 and 27-30, adding in their place a paradox of Estienne's own on lawyers; Italian names and incidents are also adapted to a French setting.

17 Alain Michel, 'Rhétorique, philosophie, christianisme: le paradoxe de la Renaissance devant les grands courants de la pensée antique', in *Le Paradoxe au temps de la Renaissance*, edited by M. T. Jones-Davies, Centre de Recherches sur la Renaissance, vol. 7 (Paris, 1982), 47-58, especially pp. 48-9 for what follows here.

18 John Donne, *Paradoxes and Problems*, edited by Helen Peters (Oxford, 1980), p. xxvi; cf. Donne's first *Paradox* which argues that all things tend towards their own extinction — a remark appropriately self-referential.

19 J. Culler, 'Paradox and the Language of Morals in La Rochefoucauld', *MLR*, LXVIII (1973), 28-39, p. 28.

20 Pierre Fontanier, *Les Figures du discours*, introduction par Gérard Genette, 'Champs' (Paris, 1968), p. 137, s.v. 'Paradoxisme'.

21 *Les Essais de Montaigne*, edited by Strowski and Gebelin, vol. III, p. 354.

22 Erasmus, ed. cit., p. 383, 491d.

23 Tournon, op. cit, p. 275.

24 Culler, art. cit., p. 29.

25 Quintilian, *Institutio oratoria*, IX. 2. 23.

26 J.-C. Margolin, 'Le Paradoxe, pierre de touche des "Jocoseria" humanistes', in *Le Paradoxe au temps de la Renaissance*, 59-84, p. 60.

27 I am not of course suggesting that all propositional paradoxes are capable of straightforward resolution. For some of the most obstinate cases, see J. L. Mackie, *Truth, Probability and Paradox: Studies in Philosophical Logic* (Oxford, 1973), pp. 290 sqq.

6

'Du repentir':
Structure and Method

James Supple

After a long period of relative neglect, 'Du repentir' has begun to receive a great deal of attention. Critical essays range from Guy Mermier's rather traditional approach[1] to Lawrence Kritzman's ultra-modern study in *Destruction/Découverte: Le Fonctionnement de la rhétorique dans les 'Essais' de Montaigne*.[2] Two very dense and detailed studies are offered by Jules Brody and François Rigolot, both of which might be said to conform to what Brody describes as a 'philological reading'.[3] More thematic studies have been provided by Marianne Meijer and myself, in which the two authors attempt to clarify the significance of III. 2 by comparing it with III. 1.[4] Two conflicting approaches are offered, however, by Bernard Croquette in his *Etude du livre III des 'Essais'* (Paris, 1985) and by Jerome Schwartz in a wide-ranging article which centres inevitably on the essay which preoccupies us today: '"La Conscience d'un homme": Reflections on the Problem of Conscience in the *Essais*'.[5] Croquette's study was written after Schwartz's paper; but there is little doubt that it represents precisely the kind of approach of which the American scholar disapproves. Whereas Croquette uses Jean-Yves Pouilloux's *Lire les 'Essais' de Montaigne* (Paris, 1969) as an authoritative starting point (pp. 8-9), Schwartz singles out Pouilloux's insistence that the *Essais* continually cast their own assertions into doubt as an example of a critical perspective which 'ignores the profoundly ethical basis of Montaigne's skepticism', and wrongly denies his work a 'certain ethical credibility' (pp. 242-3).

Those of you who are familiar with my own study of Montaigne's ethics will not be surprised to learn that I have a great deal of sympathy with Schwartz.[6] Even I am surprised, however, at his willingness to ignore the literary implications of Montaigne's enterprise. Even if Montaigne did see himself as 'a man addressing himself to men', there is no reason to conclude (despite some of his own — deliberately misleading — assertions) that he 'did not view himself as a writer at all' (p. 242). Whatever one's adherence to the various critical traditions, it seems to me, *pace* Schwartz (p. 242), to be quite right and proper — indeed, essential — that one should refuse to 'take an author's statement at face value without analyzing the nature of the communication he is engaged in'. In this respect, Croquette's approach, which is strictly contextual, is eminently preferable. He does not deny that Montaigne has opinions, but insists that 'chaque énoncé...n'est rendu possible que par les énoncés qui le précèdent et, engendré par eux, engendre à son tour d'autres énoncés, selon un mouvement qui n'a pas de fin'. I suspect, however, that he goes too far when he argues that Montaigne's arguments are *always* provisional: 'il n'avance jamais une affirmation... qui ne soit susceptible d'être aussitôt remise en question et qui ne relance la recherche dont elle procède elle-même' (pp. 9-10). He is, I think, encouraged in this because, influenced by Pouilloux, he has reverted to the traditional view that the essayist's exploration of a topic is undertaken blind: 'Montaigne explore méthodiquement des routes sans savoir où elles le conduiront, sans pouvoir deviner les chemins de traverse qui s'offriront à lui.' It is, of course, impossible to ascertain whether Montaigne knew where an essay was leading him; but I very much doubt whether Croquette's ambiguous formula ('Rien de fortuit, mais rien non plus de prémédité', p. 24) can be accurate. A study of 'Du repentir' would seem to suggest that, though Montaigne eschews (as was his wont) a rigorously ordered logical exposition, there *is* a logic behind his analysis, and that this analysis is much deeper and more methodical than Croquette seems to realise. If this view is accepted, it should be possible to develop an interpretation of 'Du repentir' which is mid-way between Croquette's and Schwartz's: less cut-and-dried than the latter; and less open-ended and (in purely thematic terms) disappointing than the former. More importantly perhaps, form and meaning will be seen to coalesce.

* * *

The opening section has been brilliantly analysed by Auerbach, who shows very well how it illustrates major themes in the *Essais* and in the rest of 'Du repentir'.[7] I will therefore pass over it now, pausing only to point out that, despite his usual display of modesty, Montaigne quickly establishes himself as an authoritative figure, given to making statements which, however paradoxical their content might be, brook no demur: 'Tant y a que je me contredits bien à l'adventure, mais la verité, comme disoit Demades, je ne la contredy point' (III. 2. 805b). We are not at all surprised, therefore, to find that he begins his analysis of repentance with an apparently incontrovertible statement: 'Il n'est vice veritablement vice qui n'offence, et qu'un jugement entier n'accuse' (806b). The unalerted sixteenth-century reader would have been only too ready to accept this at face value since it represents one of the 'creances communes' and supposedly 'legitimes' to which Montaigne has just referred. Despite the obfuscation created by original sin, medieval Catholic tradition had maintained the view that the *lumen naturale* or the *scintilla conscientiae* could generally perceive the difference between right and wrong[8] — a view reinforced by the belief of Socratic origin to which Montaigne goes on to refer: 'car [le vice] a de la laideur et incommodité si apparente, qu'à l'adventure ceux-là ont raison qui disent qu'il est principalement produict par bestise et ignorance' (*ibidem*). Montaigne then makes the connection between this view of vice and repentance clear in a striking image borrowed from his beloved Petrarch: 'Le vice laisse comme un ulcère en la chair, une repentance en l'ame, qui tousjours s'esgratigne et s'ensanglante elle mesme' (*ibidem*).

This is very reassuring since it means that even those miscreants who get away with their crimes will be punished. But Montaigne undermines the point even as he makes it. The adverbs and the impersonalised subject (the prestigious figure of Socrates is not referred to) indicate that certainty is already shading into doubt: '*à l'adventure ceux-là* ont raison qui disent qu'il est *principalement* produict par bestise et ignorance.' Worse still, Montaigne's apparently authoritative statement is circular. What is a 'vice veritablement vice'? What is a 'jugement entier'? These questions would immediately occur to anyone with a logical turn of mind. But they are inescapable for anyone who has read I. 23, where Montaigne affirms: 'Les loix de la conscience, que nous disons naistre de nature, naissent de la coustume' (I. 23. 115c).

Schwartz tries to minimise the importance of this statement by arguing that it is atypical and that it clashes with the absolute priority which Montaigne accords to the individual conscience (pp. 246-7). I am not at all sure that the apparent conflict can be overcome so easily — or that Montaigne wants us to overcome it.[9] As though reading our minds, he continues:

> Je tiens pour vices (mais chacun selon sa mesure) non seulement ceux que la raison et la nature condamnent, mais ceux aussi que l'opinion des hommes a forgé, voire fauce et erronée, si les loix et l'usage l'auctorise.
>
> (*ibidem*)

His parenthesis creates all sorts of philosophical problems which he deliberately leaves unresolved, concentrating instead on the psychological reality of repentance which, if it is sincere, will create anguish whatever its causes.

The alert reader will, however, bear these problems in mind as he watches Montaigne explore the reverse side of the coin:

> Il n'est pareillement bonté qui ne resjouysse une nature bien née. Il y a certes je ne sçay quelle congratulation de bien faire qui nous resjouit en nous mesmes,...qui accompaigne la bonne conscience.
>
> (807b)

The reference to 'une nature bien née' again makes this a circular statement;[10] 'bonté' could well be socially determined; and the deliberate vagueness ('je ne sçay quelle congratulation') leaves one wondering whether Montaigne, who was well aware of the ambiguity of our motivation,[11] is not hinting at insights which La Rochefoucauld will develop later. Whatever his own *arrière-pensées* may have been, he must have known, however, that many of his contemporaries would respond to the more positive side of his argument.[12] He does not hesitate, therefore, to use it as a platform from which to develop an idea which, as we know from other essays (notably II. 16), was dear to his heart: the superiority of the individual conscience over external opinion. Rejecting any hints of 'mixtion humaine' (II. 20. 674b), he adopts an essentialist view of human virtue, clearly stating that the individual can know whether he is being virtuous or evil ('Il n'y a que vous qui sçache si vous estes láche et cruel, ou loyal et devotieux', *ibidem*), and using his own (authoritative) example to reinforce his arguments: 'J'ay mes loix et ma court pour juger de moy, et m'y adresse plus qu'ailleurs.'

It is only at this point, when the reader has been first alerted and then lulled back into a false sense of security, that Montaigne clearly changes direction with an abrupt challenge to a 'creance commune': 'Mais ce qu'on dit, que la repentance suit de pres le peché, ne semble pas regarder le peché qui est en son haut appareil' (808b). The 'on' here could be Aristotle,[13] Seneca, who argued that the pangs of conscience prove that it is in-born,[14] contemporaries like Matthieu Coignet,[15] or even Montaigne himself, who in 'De la conscience' had apparently espoused the Epicurean view that 'Aucune cachette ne sert aux meschans…parce qu'ils ne se peuvent asseurer d'estre cachez, la conscience les descouvrant à eux mesmes' (II. 5. 367-8a). If that was his view then, he has changed it now since he goes on to emphasise the way in which vice can take permanent control of the individual who decides to espouse his sin:

> On peut desavouër et desdire les vices qui nous surprennent et vers lesquels les passions nous emportent; mais ceux qui par longue habitude sont enracinés et ancrez en une volonté forte et vigoureuse, ne sont subjects à contradiction.
>
> (*ibidem*)

This will certainly displease those who, like Juvenal, wish to argue that the sinner punishes himself ('prima est hæc ultio, quod se / Judice nemo nocens absolvitur', quoted by Montaigne, II. 5. 368a). And it looks as though worse is to come since the essayist goes on to define repentance itself in a way which suggests that it is no more than another of the vagaries of the fickle human mind: 'Le repentir n'est qu'une desditte de nostre volonté et opposition de nos fantasies, qui nous pourmene à tous sens' (*ibidem*). This is certainly intended to be provoking since Montaigne then uses the example of Horace to suggest that we can even repent of our virtue:

> Il faict desadvouër à celuy-là sa vertu passée et sa continence:
> *Quæ mens est hodie, cur eadem non puero fuit?*
> *Vel cur his animis incolumes non redeunt genæ?*

73

One should be careful to examine these statements in their context, however, before concluding like Croquette that repentance is being presented as no more than a 'coupable démission' (pp. 28-9).

To begin with, Montaigne's example of the vice which is 'enraciné …en une volonté forte et vigoureuse' proves — paradoxically — that he does not always see the will as hopelessly mobile. And, unlike the Horace he quotes here, he goes on to insist frequently on his own determination to maintain the identity between his youthful and his ageing selves (pp. 813, 816-17). More importantly still, he goes on to extol enthusiastically the value of an ordered existence: 'C'est une vie exquise, celle qui se maintient en ordre jusques en son privé' (*ibidem*). He does not make his presuppositions clear, but they will be obvious to the reader of the other essay in which Montaigne insists most clearly on the variability of the human psyche, 'De l'inconstance de nos actions' (II. 1). There, he defines wisdom in terms of the correct application of the will: 'vouloir et ne vouloir pas, tousjours, mesme chose' (332a). One surmises that he would no longer be happy about the reassuring condition which he had originally attached to this definition ('pourveu que la volonté soit juste; car, si elle n'est juste, il est impossible qu'elle soit tousjours une') since he has just indicated that experience shows that the corrupt will can be constant. One assumes too, however, that he still believes that it is possible, albeit for a minority of men, to lead a just and ordered existence. The key example given in 'Du repentir' is Socrates, to whom Brody suggests that Montaigne is, by implication, comparing himself.[16] The explicit comparison is, however, between Socrates and Alexander. The latter's most obvious function is to represent 'une vie de…riche estoffe' to which the 'vie basse et sans lustre' praised in the opening section (805b) can be compared. Socrates' self-imposed task of leading a human existence 'conformément à sa naturelle condition' also includes, however, the duty — which Alexander often failed to fulfil[17] — of living an ordered life. Hence Montaigne's conclusion: 'Le pris de l'ame ne consiste pas à aller haut, mais ordonnéement' (809b).

The problem, of course, is that Socrates, as an ideal model, is in a minority of one. Where does this leave us lesser mortals? At first sight, in a moral wilderness where 'virtuous' acts can be the result of arbitrary impulses experienced by evil men and where good men can sin just as arbitrarily: 'Comme les ames vicieuses sont incitées souvent à bien faire par quelque pulsion estrangere, aussi sont les vertueuses à faire mal' (810b). However, this is the result of a failure to ensure that moral training accords with the individual personality:

> Les inclinations naturelles s'aident et fortifient par institution; mais elles ne se changent guiere et surmontent. Mille natures, de mon temps, ont eschappé vers la vertu ou vers le vice au travers d'une discipline contraire.
>
> (*ibidem*)

Montaigne's insistence once again that the escape can be either towards vice or (more surprisingly) towards virtue is in full accord with his references earlier to those who are born with a natural tendency to good (those with a 'jugement entier' or 'une nature bien née', 806-7b) and with his implied reference to those who are not so endowed — the 'ames mal nées' referred to by Michel Magnien (see above, p. 8). I have argued elsewhere that one of Montaigne's main contributions to the sixteenth-century debate on the value of humanism is his insistence that its automatic equation of virtue with knowledge is unrealistic, that knowledge can benefit only those with an innate predisposition to virtue.[18] His point here is very similar, and equally realistic: some are born with a moral awareness, which can be developed; others are not: 'Aucuns,...pour estre colléz au vice d'une attache naturelle,...n'en trouvent [pas] la laideur' (811b). In these circumstances, it would be pointless to expect either moral improvement or sincere repentance.

The whole enterprise of moral reform is, moreover, often vitiated at source, as is exemplified, Montaigne claims, by the Protestant Reformation:

> Ceux qui ont essaié de r'aviser les meurs du monde, de mon temps, par nouvelles opinions, reforment les vices de l'apparence; ceux de l'essence, il les laissent là, s'ils ne les augmentent....
>
> (*ibidem*)

It is, furthermore, fundamentally hypocritical since it usually concentrates on superficial vices and provides an ideal excuse for giving free rein to deeper, more serious faults:

> et l'augmentation y est à craindre; on se sejourne volontiers de tout autre bien faire sur ces reformations externes arbitraires, de moindre coust et de plus grand merite; et satisfait-on par là à bon marché les autres vices naturels consubstantiels et intestins.
>
> (*ibidem*)

Hypocrisy is also found at the level of the individual, where, indeed, it is even more dangerous:

> La vraie condamnation et qui touche la commune façon de nos hommes, c'est que leur retraicte mesme est pleine de corruption et d'ordure; l'idée de leur amendement, chafourrée; leur penitence, malade et en coulpe, autant à peu près que leur peché.
>
> (*ibidem*)

Some simply do not have the necessary enlightenment to perceive their sin in the first place. Others were once aware of it, but, as a result of 'longue accoustumance', perceive it no more. Others, like Montaigne, have a judgement which is still sufficiently 'entier' (806) to make them aware of their vice, but they succumb to it anyway:

> A d'autres (duquel regiment je suis), le vice poise, mais ils le contrebalancent avec le plaisir ou autre occasion, et le souffrent et s'y prestent à certain prix: vitieusement pourtant et laschement.
>
> (811b)

It is tempting to wonder whether Montaigne's self-confessed, but unspecified, sins were sexual. But, as he does not pursue the matter, neither can we. He turns instead to a more neutral subject: the peasant from Armagnac, known as 'le larron', who openly confesses that he had shielded himself from poverty in his youth by stealing enormous quantities of agricultural produce. Having become comfortably off in his old age, he is now slowly repaying his debts and has charged his inheritors to pay off any outstanding debts should the task remain incomplete on his death (811-12). This example is of particular interest to Montaigne because it highlights the ambiguity of repentance:

> cettuy-cy regarde le larrecin comme action des-honneste et le hayt,

76

mais moins que l'indigence; s'en repent bien simplement, mais, en tant qu'elle estoit ainsi contrebalancée et compencée, il ne s'en repent pas.

(812b)

More interestingly still, it does not fit in with the categories of sin which he has established so far:

Cela, ce n'est pas cette habitude qui nous incorpore au vice et y conforme nostre entendement mesme, ny n'est ce vent impetueux qui va troublant et aveuglant à secousses nostre ame, et nous precipite pour l'heure, jugement et tout, en la puissance du vice.

(*ibidem*)

By implication, Montaigne admits that, when he sins, he too does so in full knowledge of what he is doing: 'Je fay coustumierement entier ce que je fay...mon jugement en a la coulpe ou la louange entiere; et la coulpe qu'il a une fois, il l'a tousjours' (*ibidem*). In this sense, it would seem that, far from comparing himself with the perfect Socrates, Montaigne is comparing himself with the imperfect *larron*, whose story is inserted in the middle of the essayist's discussion of himself.

This intercutting of personal and non-personal elements is not accidental and forms an essential part of the way in which Montaigne creates and transmits his message. Modern texts with paragraphs make the next transition from essayist to others clearer; but the text itself reveals the change of direction only slowly. As Montaigne continues, he could still be talking about himself:

Il y a des pechez impetueux, prompts et subits: laissons les à part. Mais en ces autres pechez à tant de fois reprins, deliberez et consultez, ou pechez de complexion...,[19] je ne puis pas concevoir qu'ils soient plantez si long temps en un mesme courage sans que la raison et la conscience de celuy qui les possede, le veuille constamment et l'entende ainsi....

(*ibidem*)

The use of 'celuy' has already created a sense of distance, however, which is soon increased as Montaigne introduces a note of understated irony: 'et le repentir qu'il se vante luy en venir à certain instant prescript, m'est un peu dur à imaginer et former' (*ibidem*). Having just admitted that he is inescapably addicted to certain sins about which, despite his disapproval, he can do nothing, Montaigne is (one might think) in no position to cast aspersions on others. But it is not their addiction to sin which upsets Montaigne (in a Christian perspective, we are all sinners); it is the claims which they falsely make to repentance:

> [B] Ils font tout à l'opposite des preceptes Stoiques, qui nous ordonnent bien de corriger les imperfections et vices que nous reconnoissons en nous, mais nous deffendent d'en estre marris et desplaisants. Ceux-cy nous font à croire qu'ils en ont grand regret et remors au dedans. Mais d'amendement et correction, [C] ny d'inter-ruption, [C] ils ne nous en font rien apparoir.
>
> (812-13)

Montaigne's reversion to discussion of his own moral attitudes has all the appearance of casual negligence ('Quant à moy...'). But it is far from casual. He has been working towards this statement from the very beginning of the essay where he describes himself as 'bien mal formé' but accepts that, in normal terms, there is no scope for improvement: 'Meshuy c'est fait' (804b):

> Quant à moy, je puis desirer en general estre autre; je puis condam-ner et me desplaire de ma forme universelle, et supplier Dieu pour mon entiere reformation et pour l'excuse de ma foiblesse naturelle. Mais cela, je ne le doits nommer repentir, ce me semble....
>
> (813b)

It has been argued that Montaigne 'admits in a roundabout way that he does not repent',[20] but such arguments take little or no account of his strategy in this essay. His (in Catholic eyes) deliberately provocative and strikingly memorable introduction to the debate on repentance ('Excusons icy ce que je dy souvent que je me repens rarement', 806b) can be correctly interpreted only in the light of the developments to which it leads, and not least in the light of his later definition of repentance: 'Si la repentance pesoit sur le plat de la balance, elle en-porteroit le peché' (813b). When he writes (811b): 'A d'autres (duquel regiment je suis) *le vice poise*', he expects that statement to be read in the context of subsequent statements concerning his regret at his imperfect condition ('je puis condamner et *me desplaire* de ma forme universelle', 813b). When he writes, in the same context, 'je ne puis faire mieux', one should assume, I think, that he is referring to real but failed attempts to overcome the sin that distresses him. That this failure does not lead to ostentatious displays of breast-beating should not surprise us. In purely human terms, Montaigne's character is such that he is unlikely to nourish any internal divisions (812). In theological terms, moral failure is to be expected from all but the most saintly ('Mes actions sont reglées et conformes à ce que je suis et à ma condition')[21] and is an inescapable consequence of original sin: 'Ce n'est pas macheure, c'est plustost une teinture universelle qui me tache' (813b).

I was going to write: 'We have stumbled here upon a thorny subject: Montaigne's religion.' But such a claim to casual organisation would but mirror Montaigne's own *neglegentia diligens*: like Montaigne, I have been working towards this problem, which, in the context of repentance, is inescapable. It would be nice if we could escape it since it is the cause of so much disagreement among critics. Dreano and Sclafert seemed to have established that Montaigne was not the unbeliever that Gide had pretended; but Richard Sayce and Dorothy Coleman have modified their conclusions, placing the emphasis firmly back on the more sceptical side of his approach to Christianity.[22] Though not specifically analysing Montaigne's religion, Carol Clark has also argued with reference to 'Du repentir' that 'It becomes fairly clear in this essay...that [Montaigne] is deeply suspicious of the whole Christian notion of repentance'.[23] Malcolm Smith, on the other hand, has seen in III. 2 further proof of his contention that Montaigne was a good Catholic, anxious to ensure that his views conformed with the decrees of the Council of Trent.[24] We have seen that Montaigne attacks the Protestants (above, pp. 75-6); but I can see no reason to believe that he is excluding bad Catholics when he questions the way in which hypocritical religious faith is used to mask moral failings: 'Je ne trouve aucune qualité si aysée à contrefaire que la devotion, si on n'y conforme les meurs et la vie' (813b). When he criticises the man who falsely claims to repent 'à certain instant prescript' (812b), I suspect, too, that he is referring to those who seek absolution only at Easter. On the other hand, I feel like M. A. Screech that one should take Montaigne seriously when he argues that he rarely repents because true repentance involves a spiritual enlightenment which can be granted only by grace.[25] Unless we are prepared to accept that Montaigne is deliberately setting out to deceive us, we must believe him when he writes:

> Je ne cognoy pas de repentance superficielle, moyenne et de ceremonie. Il faut...qu'elle pinse mes entrailles et les afflige autant profondement que Dieu me voit, et autant universellement;
>
> (813b)

and when he specifically refers to the need for divine grace: 'Il faut que Dieu nous touche le courage' (816b). To invert Dorothy Coleman's quip, I am inclined to argue that Montaigne was, in this area at least, a wayward Catholic, but a good Christian![26]

Marianne Meijer has already made a similar point in an article where she shows that Montaigne, who is evidently insisting on full contrition, is rejecting the Catholic Church's pronouncements on the value of the weaker but, in its view, still useful attrition.[27] It is, I think, this which leads Montaigne to end the essay by diverting our attention away from the main theological issue as, in an apparently off-handed manner, he introduces the much less contentious themes of practical mis-calculations ('*Quant aux negoces*, il m'est eschappé plusieurs bonnes aventures à faute d'heureuse conduitte', 813b) and the moral decline induced by old age: '*Au demeurant*, je hay cet accidental repentir que l'aage apporte' (815b). There is still a strategy at work, of course. Since errors of a practical nature are inevitable from time to time and since old age is bound to dull one's faculties, Montaigne can be sure of taking us with him when he argues that wisdom lies in lucid acceptance of our limitations — in which case, we will be less likely to question one of his main contentions (that 'le repentir ne touche pas proprement les choses qui ne sont pas en nostre force', 813b).

Montaigne has not, in any case, lost sight of his original starting point concerning the relationship between virtue and knowledge, which he has been subtly modifying during the course of the essay. One can easily conceive more virtuous life-styles, he tells us, but there will always remain a huge gap between the concept and the reality:

J'imagine infinies natures plus hautes et plus reglées que la mienne; je n'amande pourtant mes facultez: comme ny mon bras, ny mon esprit ne deviennent plus vigoreux pour en *concevoir* un autre qui le soit. Si d'*imaginer* et desirer un agir plus noble que le nostre produisoit la repentance du nostre, nous aurions à nous repentir de nos operations plus innocentes: d'autant que nous *jugeons* bien qu'en la nature plus excellente elles auroyent esté conduites d'une plus grande perfection....

(813b)

Where old age is concerned, on the other hand, it is important to remain as lucid as possible:

Il ne nous faut pas laisser emporter si entiers aux alterations naturelles, que d'en *abastardir nostre jugement*. La jeunesse et le plaisir n'ont pas faict autrefois que j'aie *m'escogneu* le visage du vice en la volupté; ny ne faict à cette heure le degoust que les ans m'apportent, que je *mescognoisse* celuy de la volupté au vice.

(815b)

This is why Montaigne rejects the 'accidental repentir que l'aage apporte' (815b), insisting that, without correct knowledge of vice ('La volupté n'en est en soy ny pasle ny descolorée, pour estre aperceuë par des yeux chassieux'), there can be no virtue: 'On ne peut se vanter de mespriser et combatre la volupté, *si on ne la voit, si on l'ignore*' (816b). As usual with Montaigne, nothing is simple. In the realm of practical miscalculations, one has to accept decisions based on limited knowledge (813-14). In the realm of ethics, lucidity is the essential precondition for the attainment of true virtue. But it is not, even here, an automatic recipe for virtuous conduct: one can see one's vice without being necessarily able to repent of it; and one can conceive nobler, more honourable behaviour without being able to imitate it. Yet, lucid acceptance of one's inescapable imperfections is an essential requirement if one is to avoid pointless or, worse still, hypocritical self-recriminations: '*Je ne me flatte pas*: à circonstances pareilles, je seroy tousjours tel' (813b).

By referring back to his previous practical errors and forward to the increased physical, mental, and moral decline which will be brought on

81

by old age, Montaigne also gives himself the opportunity to complete his analysis of a philosophical and moral problem which threatens to make repentance impossible: the continuing identity, or lack of it, of the individual. As Jerome Schwartz rightly points out:

> Time renders conscience problematic....Conscience flows as time flows, as intention, act, and reflection succeed one another diachronically. How then is it possible to assess motive and intention retrospectively, since the 'I' of the intention, the 'I' of the act, and the 'I' of reflection can never be precisely the same?
>
> (p. 269)

François Rigolot is, in my view, wrong, however, to extract isolated statements from 'Du repentir' and to conclude:

> En tant qu'il implique un 'désaveu' du passé..., le repentir est une attitude anti-naturelle vis-à-vis de l'écoulement de la vie, de la fluidité de l'existence. Se repentir, ce serait en somme tenter de remonter la *pente* du temps, chercher *l'être* au lieu d'accepter *le passage*: 'Je ne peints pas l'estre. Je peints le passage.'
>
> (p. 123)

Montaigne certainly emphasises the instablity of the human psyche, and (indeed) of his own: 'ce ne sont que mousches et atomes qui promeinent ma volonté' (814b); but this is not seen as a desirable norm in III. 2 any more than it is in II. 1.[28] Nothing is totally constant, and it would be folly to hope that it could be (804-5); but our inconstancy can be exaggerated or attenuated by our own mental behaviour. Like Horace, whom he quotes to very different effect in 'De la conscience', Montaigne disapproves of the vast majority of mankind, which simply gives itself up to the whims of the passing moment: 'Quod petiit, spernit; repetit quod nuper omisit; / Æstuat, et vitae disconvenit ordine toto' (II. 1. 333a). It is to such as these that he is referring when he describes repentance in such a reductive way: 'une desditte de nostre volonté...qui nous pourmene à tous sens' (808b). For his own part, he does not hesitate to claim that his own variablity can be extremely limited: 'De moy, je ne me sens guere agiter par secousse...Si je ne suis chez moy, j'en suis tousjours bien pres' (811b). He insists, too, on the identity

82

which exists between his earlier self and his self now: 'en matiere d'opinions universelles, dés l'enfance je me logeay au poinct où j'avois à me tenir' (812b); 'Lors que je consulte des deportemens de ma jeunesse avec ma vieillesse, je trouve que je les ay communement conduits avec ordre, selon moy' (813b). He knows that increasing old age will in all probability get the better of him (817); but is steadfast in his desire to maintain his identity: 'Je ne me suis pas attendu d'attacher monstrueusement la queuë d'un philosophe à la teste d'un homme perdu' (816c).

It is this commitment to one's own identity which, as Marcel Conche has shown, *creates* our identity, especially in the moral domain.[29] This identity has, of necessity, to take into account our inescapable shortcomings ('Si j'avois à revivre, je revivrois comme j'ay vescu', 816c); but it does not exclude the possibility of sincere repentance: 'et si ay des ravisemens sains et vigoureux' (811b). These 'ravisemens', unlike those imposed by those who seek to 'r'aviser les meurs du monde' (*ibidem*), have to be freely accepted by the individual; and, above all, they have to be sincere: 'Je ne cognoy pas de repentance superficielle, moyenne et de ceremonie. Il faut...qu'elle pinse mes entrailles et les afflige autant profondement que Dieu me voit, et autant universellement' (813b). Departing from Montaigne's own practice, I have quoted this passage twice. I do so partly because of its intrinsic importance (it shows that, when Montaigne says 'je me repens rarement', he means that he can rarely achieve *deep* repentance, not that repentance is of no importance to him) and partly because of the light which it casts on the concept of the 'jugement entier' with which he began his analysis of the problems posed by sin. Ultimately, it is only God who can permanently possess an unclouded judgement, see sin, and immediately condemn it. A complete transformation of the sinner's personality (what Michael Screech calls 'repentance by which a man sees his whole life and his whole person as through the eyes of God')[30] can be achieved only through grace: 'Il faut que Dieu nous touche le courage.' Without that grace, all we can aim at is a relative but nonetheless essential improvement both in our lucidity and in our honesty: 'Il faut que nostre conscience s'amende d'elle mesme par renforcement de nostre raison' (816b).

One could go on isolating facets of what, in traditional terms, might be called 'Montaigne's concept of repentance'. Enough has been said, I hope, to show that this concept is not as haphazardly worked out or as tentative as Croquette suggests. But it is by no means as static or as unambiguous as Schwartz seems to believe. It certainly cannot be determined by simply extracting individual statements from the *Essais* and attempting to determine whether they are 'typical' or 'atypical'. Montaigne's statements form part of a literary structure which, quite apart from its own intrinsic value, enables Montaigne to pursue his analyses in greater depth, to develop, modify, or contradict his apparent *prises de position*, to create tensions between them, and to ensure that one statement casts light on another. Form and meaning are one: 'qui touche l'un, touche l'autre' (806b).

NOTES

1 'L'Essai "Du repentir" de Montaigne', *French Review*, XLI (1967-8), 485-92.
2 Lexington, 1980, 126-38.
3 Brody, '"Du repentir" (III. 2): A Philological Reading', *Yale French Studies*, LXIV (1983), 238-72; Rigolot, 'La *Pente* du "repentir": un exemple de remotivation du signifiant dans les *Essais* de Montaigne', in *Columbia Montaigne Conference Papers*, edited by D. M. Frame and Mary B. McKinley (Lexington, 1981), 119-34.
4 Meijer, 'De l'honnête, de l'utile et du repentir', *Journal of Medieval and Renaissance Studies*, XII (1982), 259-74; Supple, '"Excusons icy ce que je dy souvent": The Relationship between "Du repentir" and "De l'utile et de l'honneste"', to appear in *Forum for Modern Language Studies*.
5 For Schwartz, see *Essays on Montaigne in Honor of Donald M. Frame*, edited by R. C. La Charité (Lexington, 1977), 242-76.
6 *Arms versus Letters: The Military and Literary Ideal in the 'Essais' of Montaigne* (Oxford, 1984).
7 *Mimesis*, translated by W. Trask (New York, 1957), pp. 249-73.
8 See Marcel Conche, *Montaigne et la philosophie* (Paris, 1987), pp. 120-1; and Schwartz, art. cit., pp. 247-50.
9 See Richard Sayce, *The Essays of Montaigne: A Critical Exploration* (London, 1972), p. 197.
10 See John Holyoake, 'Montaigne and the Concept of "bien né"', *BHR*, XXX (1968), 483-98.

11 See Conche, op. cit., pp. 121-2.

12 See J. Haight, *The Concept of Reason in French Classical Literature, 1635-1690* (Toronto, 1982), pp. 13, 25; also F. Copleston, *A History of Philosophy*, vol. III, part 2 (New York, 1963), p. 33.

13 See Rigolot, art. cit., p. 129.

14 Schwartz, art. cit., p. 149.

15 *Instruction aux princes pour garder la foy promise* (Paris, 1577), p. 341.

16 See Brody, art. cit., pp. 249 sqq.

17 See Supple, *Arms versus Letters*, p. 211.

18 *Ibidem*, pp. 99-105.

19 Montaigne's C insertion ('voire pechez de profession et de vacation') is more evidently applicable to others.

20 Sayce, op. cit., p. 220.

21 See, on 'la marmaille d'hommes que nous sommes', Michael Screech's excellent *Montaigne and Melancholy: The Wisdom of the Essays* (London, 1983), pp. 134-6.

22 Sayce, op. cit., pp. 202-32; Coleman, *Montaigne's Essays* (London, 1987), pp. 49-65.

23 *The Web of Metaphor* (Lexington, 1978), p. 87.

24 *Montaigne and the Roman Censors* (Geneva, 1981), pp. 67-9.

25 Screech, op. cit., pp. 46-51.

26 'Montaigne was very much a Roman Catholic but not a Christian', review of Screech's *Montaigne and Melancholy*, in *French Studies*, XXXVIII (1984), p. 195.

27 Art. cit., pp. 266-7.

28 'Si par discours nous entreprenions certaine voie, nous la prendrions la plus belle' (II. 1. 332-3a).

29 Conche, op. cit., pp. 118-19.

30 Screech, op. cit., p. 49.

7

Serious Frivolity?
Word-Play in the *Essais*

Keith Cameron

No reader of the *Essais* can fail to be aware of Montaigne's evident dexterity in the use of words and his predilection for word-play. Dorothy Coleman recently observed that:

> Throughout the *Essais*, [Montaigne's] delight in manipulating language is evident; puns, paradoxes, innuendoes, innovation in making up words, in using quite coarse terms like 'le catze', irony, comic sarcasm, the imagery which is often 'poetic' in that it sheds light on obscure parts of our activities or brain-movements.[1]

Montaigne's linguistic gymnastics have been considered by a number of scholars and, on the whole, they share the view that Richard Sayce expressed:

> ...in Montaigne, and this is what distinguishes him from most of his euphuistic or mannerist contemporaries, such devices are never merely verbal tricks...this playfulness can be overstressed and should not blind us to the underlying seriousness.[2]

The changing attitudes towards the pun led the austere abbé F. X. Talbert in 1744 to note, in his *Eloge de Montaigne*, with something approaching embarrassment:

> il y a quelquefois des jeux de mots; il dit de Tacite: *Il nous peint et nous pince.* Il appelle la mort le *bout*, et non *le but de la vie*; mais ce défaut puéril est fort rare chez lui.[3]

In the sixteenth century, however, word-play was considered to be an important rhetorical ingredient in the art of story-telling. Thomas Wilson, in his *Arte of Rhetorique* of 1553, argues that:

> And now bicause our senses be suche, that in hearyng a right wholsome matter, wee either fall a slepe, when we should moste harken, or els are weried with stil hearyng one thyng, without any change, and thinke that the best part of his tale, resteth in makyng an ende: the wittie and learned have used delitefull saiynges, and quicke sentences ever emong their weightie causes, consideryng that not onely good wil is got therby (for what is he that loveth not mirth?) but also men wounder at suche a head, as hath mennes hartes at his commaundement, beyng able to make theim merie when he list, and that by one worde speakyng, either in answeryng some thyng spoken before, or els oftentymes, in gevyng the onset, beyng not provoked thereunto. Again we se that men are full oft abashed, and putte out of countenaunce, by suche tauntyng meanes, and those that have so dooen, are compted to be fine men, and pleasaunt felowes, suche, as fewe dare set foote with them.[4]

Admittedly, the emphasis in this passage is upon speech rather than writing, but Montaigne himself insists, volubly and repeatedly, that he has introduced the tone of conversation into the *Essais*. The whole of the first chapter of the third book deals with the problem of speech and giving one's word.[5] Within its opening lines he informs us:

> Je parle au papier comme je parle au premier que je rencontre. Qu'il soit vray, voicy dequoy.
>
> (III. 1. 790b)

He creates the impression that he wants to abandon rhetoric and be 'himself', yet as has been shown, by so doing he follows certain well-established rhetorical conventions.[6]

The desire to introduce 'improvisation' into his writing was certainly not restricted to Montaigne. As Terence Cave writes:

> the 'colloquial' mode is of the greatest significance for vernacular writing in sixteenth-century France. The fictions of Rabelais and

Marguerite de Navarre, the quasi-dialogic movement of Montaigne's *Essais*, all attempt to escape the space of the written text, to disrupt it or open it up, while yet retaining fragments of writing consecrated by tradition as an integral part of their movement.[7]

Even when Montaigne defends his use of 'un mot du creu de Gascoingne' (III. 5. 875b) by asking 'Est-ce pas ainsi que je parle par tout? me represente-je pas vivement?' (*ibidem*), he is following a precept enunciated by Guazzo in *The Civile Conversation*:

> ...as money, by meane of the coine hath a publicke stampe set upon it, whereby it is known where it was made, so our speech ought to have a mark upon it, which may shewe the originality and countrie of him that speaketh.[8]

The desire of Montaigne to give a colloquial flavour to his book is made even more evident by the editorial habit of indicating the various additions to the *Essais*. A quick perusal, for example, of the C additions to the third book yields a large number of cases where Montaigne introduces into the body of the already lively edition of 1588 a multitude of phrases and expressions in which word-play is apparent. His use of pithy expressions, of colloquial sayings, his ironic turn of phrase, his sarcasm, have all helped to give the reader a glimpse of Montaigne's humour, a humour which was noted by his contemporary Estienne Pasquier and later by Pascal[9] as well as by more recent critics:

> Avec ses paradoxes et ses bizarreries, ses contradictions et ses antithèses, ses interrogations et ses flottements, avec ses fréquents jeux de mots, l'essai montaignien ressortit à l'imaginaire. Si l'humour a prescrit à l'essai une manière de dire, l'humour lui a imposé son ambiguïté essentielle pour en faire un genre original qui emprunte à la philosophie son goût pour l'abstrait et le général, à la littérature sa préférence pour le concret et le particulier.[10]

What I have endeavoured to establish so far is that Montaigne's use of word-play reflects his intent to give a colloquial framework to the *Essais*, thereby following a contemporary tradition visible amongst the humanists, and that, in his case, the word-play often creates a humorous effect. Yet Montaigne cannot really be considered to be a humanist in the sense that Rabelais and Erasmus were humanists. They were scholars and he was well-read. Although those who read Montaigne for pleasure have no hesitation in declaring an awareness of his sense of humour, there does seem to be a desire to defend all that Montaigne has written as being an illustration of his keen stylistic awareness, of his cunning intelligence, of a constant manifestation of his profundity. I share many of these views, but I feel that we should exercise greater restraint over accepting all that he has written as being an example of rhetorical craftiness, whether it be 'natural' or school rhetoric. Montaigne presumably knew himself very well and he appears to have been aware of his own defects. Do we always have to think that any apparently disparaging remark he makes must be interpreted as a case of false modesty? It is surely not purely for self-defence or out of false modesty that he writes that:

> On me pourroit tenir pour sage en telle condition de sagesse que je tien pour sottise.
>
> (III. 5. 847c)

He warns us that he sometimes is subject to exaggeration, being somewhat partial to hyperbole:

> La parole vive et bruyante, comme est la mienne ordinaire, s'emporte volontiers à l'hyperbole.
>
> (III. 11. 1028c)

He admits that he sometimes does not believe his ears when he comes out with certain remarks:

> [B] je hasarde souvent des boutades de mon esprit, desquelles je me deffie, [C] et certaines finesses verbales, dequoy je secoue les oreilles.
>
> (III. 8. 943)

> (cf. Florio's translation: 'I often hazard upon certaine outslips of my minde, for which I distruste my selfe; and certaine verball wilie-beguilies, whereat I shake mine eares.'[11])

and yet, he does not retract them as they can be considered praiseworthy and may encounter public approval:

[B] mais je les laisse courir à l'avanture. [C] Je voys qu'on s'honore de pareilles choses. Ce n'est pas à moy seul d'en juger. (cf. Florio: 'but I let them runne at hab or nab; I see some honour themselves with such like things; T'is not for me alone to judge of them.')

Is it coincidental that these statements, referring to the colloquial/ familiar aspect of his style, are all C additions? In 'Sur des vers de Virgile' when on the subject of health, he describes a state of mind or 'humour' which accompanies good health:

Ce feu de gayeté suscite en l'esprit des eloises vives et claires, outre nostre portée naturelle et entre les enthousiasmes les plus gaillards, si non les plus esperdus. Or bien ce n'est pas merveille si un contraire estat affesse mon esprit, le clouë et faict un effect contraire.

(III. 5. 844c)

Is Montaigne not describing here a state of being which good health brings, of both physical and intellectual excitement? The feeling of bubbling over, of being hyperfluent in thought, of exhilaration revealing itself in thought associations, word and sound associations, the 'boutades d'esprit', the 'finesses verbales', the 'parole vive et bruyante'? It is perhaps this awareness of how his mind can sometimes work that prompted Montaigne to warn us about the personal and not prescriptive nature of what he says:

Car en ce que je dy, je ne pleuvis autre certitude, sinon que c'est ce que lors j'en avoy en ma pensée, pensée tumultuaire et vacillante. C'est par manière de devis que je parle de tout, et de rien par maniere d'advis.

(III. 11. 1033c)

We must not forget too that that liberty, that absence of constraint which Montaigne sees as so important in educating a child, is also visible in his attitude towards his own style and towards 'wisdom':

> J'ayme une sagesse gaye et civile, et fuis l'aspreté des meurs et
> l'austerité, ayant pour suspecte toute mine rebarbative.
>
> (III. 5. 844b)

He craves a certain freedom of expression, a freedom which will include
pleasantries, and yet he is constantly aware that on occasion he
oversteps the mark. As for pleasantries, we have examples of wit in the
form of an aphorism as in the opening sentences of III. 1:

> Personne n'est exempt de dire des fadaises. Le malheur est de les
> dire curieusement.
>
> (III. 1. 790b)

or at the beginning of III. 7:

> Puisque nous ne la pouvons aveindre, vengeons nous à en mesdire.
>
> (III. 7. 916b)

As I read through Montaigne's additions to the third book, I get the
impression that although he tells us his 'ouvrage' should be considered
as a 'registre de durée' (II. 18. 665c), he was also trying to effect a
'Euphues' on his text and to add sentences which, albeit noble and
apparently relevant, are there to show his stylistic, linguistic awareness
and, very often, are a mere tribute to Montaigne's wit.

In III. 2, for example, the first C addition finishes with repetitive play
on 'se plaindre de quoy':

> Si le monde se plaint de quoy je parle trop de moy, je me plains de
> quoy il ne pense seulement pas à soy.
>
> (III. 2. 805c)

The next substantive addition ends on a sentence where 'sçavant' and
'suffisant' are opposed:

> Un personage sçavant n'est pas sçavant par tout; mais le suffisant

est par tout suffisant, et à ignorer mesme.

(806)

The next consists of a rather pompous, high-flown rhetorical play on 'conscience':

> ma conscience se contente de soy: non comme de la conscience d'un
> ange ou d'un cheval, mais comme de la conscience d'un homme.
>
> (*ibidem*)

Not one of these additions, memorable though they may be, really adds a great deal to what Montaigne has already written. They appear a little slick, to be there as phonic interplay, they have the subtle, clever balance of an aphorism and thus linger long in our minds and end up by pushing the context into the background and thus distort our reading of the *Essais*.

A little further along in the same chapter, a long C addition finishes with a play on 'failli':

> je n'eusse guere failly de faillir plus tost que de bien faire à leur
> mode.
>
> (807)

Two pages later, the whole of the C addition seems to be an excuse for Montaigne to juxtapose, somewhat wittily and appositely, two appearances of the word 'gloire', which Florio highlights by putting in italics:

> La plus courte façon d'arriver à la gloire, ce seroit faire par
> conscience ce que nous faisons pour la gloire.
>
> (809)

Similarly, the next addition begins with a play on 'grandeur':

> Sa grandeur ne s'exerce pas en la grandeur, c'est en la mediocrité.
>
> (*ibidem*)

93

In fact there seems to be a pattern which emerges in the construction of many of the C additions. When word-play is involved, it either constitutes the *raison d'être* of the addition, sometimes creating a play upon a word in the already existing text, or it is used in the initial sentence, or the addition leads up to a sentence containing word-play, thus conferring upon the whole addition a certain epigrammatic twist.

'Sur des vers de Virgile' provides some good examples:

Raison d'être

je naturaliserois l'art autant comme ils artialisent la nature (874)

[about Plutarch] je ne le puis si peu racointer que je n'en tire cuisse ou aile (875)

Sommes nous pas bien bruttes de nommer brutale l'operation qui nous faict? (878)

Trouves tu que tu sois trop à ton aise, si ton aise ne te vient à desplaisir? (879)

An addition which creates word-play on a word in the already existing text

[B]...et honteuses les parties qui y servent [i.e. à la production de l'homme] [C] (asteure sont les miennes proprement honteuses et peneuses) (878)

Additions which start with word-play

Il est des effects qui peuvent perdre sans impudicité leur pudicité (867)

Ne semble ce pas estre une humeur lunatique de la Lune (882)

Et ce germe de beauté naissante ne se laisse manier à mains (894)

Those which lead up to word-play

> que la coustume rende indecent et nuisible qu'on communique à
> persone tout ce qu'on en sçait et qu'on en sent (870)

> toutes gens fanatiques qui pensent honnorer leur nature en se
> desnaturant, qui se prisent de leur mespris, et s'amendent de leur
> empirement (879)

Such additions when read as an integral part of the text are absorbed by
the surrounding context, but when aligned, the impressive use of
word-play in the C additions becomes apparent.

I am aware of the use of word-play as an indication of an author's
Weltanschauung :

> La figure étymologique dévoile la manière unique de Montaigne, sa
> vision du monde, qui est en même temps lyrique et ironique, c'est à
> dire intime et réservée.[12]

I am equally aware that word-play draws our attention to the arbitrary
nature of language:

> Le jeu de mots est en fait un croc-en-jambe aux mécanismes
> linguistiques, et par là même met en cause le caractère référentiel du
> langage articulé en montrant la nature arbitraire du signe
> linguistique.[13]

And yet, in spite of this awareness and a realisation that these criteria
can be applied, often profitably, to the *Essais*, I am convinced that
frequently Montaigne has sought to encapsulate his thought in a
resonant manner not so much to reveal a new aspect of his thought as
with the express intention of enlivening his text. But why? Was it
because he wanted the *Essais* not only to serve as a compendium of his
mental evolution, but also to contain aspects of his own natural gaiety
and therefore to become a collection of his own *bons mots*? He may
indicate this when, again on the subject of his health, he tells us in

another C addition to 'De l'experience' how he seeks consolation from his medical jottings:

> si quelque estonnement me menace, feuilletant ces petits brevets descousus comme des feuilles Sybyllines, je ne faux plus de trouver où me consoler de quelque prognostique favorable en mon experience passée.
>
> (III. 13. 1092c)

Given the parallel he establishes between physical and mental health, this could be the case. Yet, on the other hand, in another C addition, this time to 'De la vanité', Montaigne, talking about changes to his book, refers to such changes as 'quelque embleme supernumeraire' (III. 9. 964c), which refers to the emblem or ornament used in marquetry and here accompanied by 'supernumeraire' could be interpreted as superfluous or more likely supralinguistic, i.e. giving an overall tone to the work. He does go on to say:

> Ce ne sont que surpoids, qui ne condamnent point la premiere forme, mais donnent quelque pris particulier à chacune des suivantes par une petite subtilité ambitieuse.
>
> (*ibidem*)

This suggests his conscious desire to be 'subtil', to demonstrate his wit. He is aware, however, of the phenomenon of being a 'poet and not knowing it', for in a C addition to 'Du parler prompt ou tardif' (I. 10), we read:

> J'aurai eslancé quelque subtilité en escrivant...je l'ay si bien perdue que je ne sçay ce que j'ay voulu dire: et l'a l'estranger descouverte par fois avant moy.
>
> (I. 10. 40c)

Now are we to believe that many of the subtleties which exist in the *Essais* are there as spontaneous manifestations of Montaigne's wit? At times they cause us to ponder over their meaning for too long for us just to accept them as mere *boutades*. Do they not often reveal a tendency to be rather glib, remarks which have been made in a state of hyper-excitement and are not really very profound? Let us return, however, to the 'petites subtilités ambitieuses'. Was Montaigne's aim in the *Essais* merely to convey, by introducing widespread word-play, the impression of the spontaneity of conversation? His own caveats as to the interpretation of his 'subtilités' should make us pause. Is he not saying: 'Sometimes my tongue runs away with me and you should not pay too much attention to what I have written'? Is he not saying: 'Sometimes I write things because I like the way it sounds as much as what it means'? Is he not suggesting that he is trying to make the *Essais* more agreeable for the reader? It *is* also true that the word-play arrests the attention of the reader. It makes him ponder the unusual association of words or sounds.

In the same C addition referred to above, Montaigne goes on to refer to the chronology of his 'contes' (III. 9. 964c) which, because of his method of inserting them in the text, are not in strict order of occurrence. Now why does he refer to 'contes'? Is he speaking of his exempla, his anecdotes? or is he not here revealing a more fundamental attitude towards his book?

In a stimulating article, Gabriel-André Pérouse set out his theory that the form of the *Essais* owes much to the form of contemporary stories, the *nouvelles*.[14] He gives a synopsis of the history of the *nouvelle* in the 1580s, emphasising the fact that the characteristic feature of fiction at this time was the 'discours bigarré':

> après avoir, un temps, affecté un visage carrément romanesque, la voici [i.e. la vieille littérature de la vie sociale] redevenue, pour une très large part, conversation, expression du quotidien d'une société; mais d'une société reconnaissable. Elle a quitté la campagne pour la ville, et s'est mise à l'école des libraires. Maintenant, sous la forme disgracieuse du discours bigarré, elle est tout à la fois, facétie, cadre pour histoires tragiques ou comiques, forum pour les débats d'idées, tribune; on voit même s'y glisser la méditation personnelle. Ces difformités se condamnent elles-mêmes.
>
> (p. 34)

Could it not be that Montaigne in his conception of his work adopted an approach similar to that of D'Aubigné in *Les Tragiques*? — that is they took a form, the short story or the epic poem, both based on fiction, and composed a new, authentic story and epic poem based upon their own experience, the supreme opposition of nature versus art.

It is certain there are many similarities between the conception of time in the fictional literature of the 1580s and that espoused by Montaigne.[15] Montaigne reveals on many an occasion his appreciation of the 'gallic salt' and verbal humour which play such an important role in fictional literature. In my earlier quotations, Terence Cave mentioned the widespread use of the colloquial mode in fictional literature and Richard Sayce sought to make a distinction between Montaigne and his contemporaries. Sayce draws attention to the stylistic similarity that exists between John Lyly's *Euphues* of 1579 and the word-play in the *Essais*. *Euphues* is symptomatic of a tendency in contemporary European literature; the extensive use of word-play to enhance a text is to be found both in fictional literature and in so-called serious work, in the works of D'Aubigné, Sponde, Donne, to name but a few, only to fall from fashion and favour at the beginning of the seventeenth century.

Montaigne's style was well appreciated by his contemporaries; the wit, Estienne Tabourot, published a *huitain* in his honour in 1588 in which he shows his admiration:

> Quiconque voit la nette purité
> De tes escrits, les lit de tel courage
> Que si c'estoit quelque gentil ouvrage
> Qu'il eut jadis luy-mesme medité:
> Puis tout ravi de sa simplicité,
> Recognoissant ton style inimitable
> T'adore ainsi qu'une divinité,
> Te voyant seul à toymesme semblable.[16]

Tabourot highlights Montaigne's mastery at combining 'simplicité' and 'gentillesse' in writing the sort of book that others had contemplated. But what others?

In that same year Tabourot had also brought out a new edition of *Les Bigarrures* with Jean Richer, the same publisher used by Montaigne for the first Parisian edition of the *Essais*.[17] Furthermore, Tabourot had included in the so-called *Quatrieme Livre* (in reality, the second book) of

Les Bigarrures, dated 1585 (published by Jean Richer), four chapters written in the 'ton des *Essais* de Montaigne'.[18] This suggests not only admiration for Montaigne but also a certain ambivalence in Tabourot's mind with regard to certain forms of writing. It is obvious that there is a great deal of 'contamination' between Montaigne and the contemporary authors of fiction. The significance of this *rapprochement* should lie in *our* attitude towards Montaigne's attitude towards his work.

Although it may well be a 'livre consubstantiel à son autheur' (II. 18. 665c), the book assumes a value as a creative text in its own right; not the value of an autobiographical work but one which is closer to that of a fictional text. It would be more productive for readers to consider the *Essais* as an autobiographical novel, a text to which the author could return and which he could embellish, to which he could add remarks which not only provided clarity or profundity to what he had written, but also a touch of necessary frivolity.

Barbara Bowen has pointed out how 'both *escrits* and *paroles* are dependent upon rhetoric, and...the rules of *escrits* and those of *paroles* are interchangeable'.[19] Many of the additions which have a serious ring to them (Florio does not pick up all of the plays upon words, sounds, etc.) should perhaps be considered as having been produced with a frivolous intent. This intent is no longer always apparent in the printed text because the ironic note would only sound if the text were read aloud, being produced by the inflexion of the voice, the change in intonation and accent. We should not forget that Montaigne was particularly sensitive to such supralinguistic factors:

> L'occasion, la compaignie, le branle mesme de ma voix, tire plus de mon esprit, que je n'y trouve lors que je le sonde et employe à part moy.
>
> (I. 10. 40b)

'A quel propos, en voustre advis, tend ce prelude et coup d'essay?'[20] It seems to me that we may attribute too much force to these pithy sayings, that we should be more wary of word-play in the *Essais*. Our interpretation of Montaigne's thought should not allow itself to depend upon phrases involving intricate word-play. Such phrases, by their very formation, tend to twist logical reasoning to fit in with their phonic and morphemic structure. Such phrases should always be treated *cum grano salis*, thought-provoking though they may be.

Consider the following:

> Mais il m'est advis que c'est bien le bout, non pourtant le but de la vie.
>
> (III. 12. 1051c)

Our first reaction might be to take 'but' in the sense of 'aim' rather than 'purpose', cf. Florio: 'But me thinks, it is indeede the end, yet not the scope of life.' And yet how are we to interpret this in the light of another C addition?

> Qui apprendroit les hommes à mourir, leur apprendroit à vivre.
>
> (I. 20. 90c)

And does not his addition to III. 1:

> La perfidie peut estre en quelque cas excusable: lors seulement elle l'est, qu'elle s'employe à punir et trahir la perfidie.
>
> (III. 1. 797c)

appear to condone perfidy (Florio translates it by 'treason') in certain circumstances? Yet, on the previous page, his attitude is somewhat condemning towards Pomponius Flaccus.

We should not in our serious, academic pursuit of the interpretation of the wisdom of the *Essais* overlook the playful, occasionally irresponsible, if not always immediately detectable, element in Montaigne's work. We are probably the source of a great deal of merriment for Montaigne if he is able to witness our analyses of his thought. We should remember not to make his 'finesse trop fine' (III. 1. 795b). And yet this may be all part of his great intention. Are we to believe that Montaigne is making us a party to his own game? Is it 'un jeu qui n'exclut pas une certaine gravité puisque c'est la sagesse qui en est le but. Le jeu n'écarte pas l'enjeu'?[21] Is it a question of serious frivolity, seriousness, or mere frivolity? How can any analysis of Montaigne be anything but paradoxical?

NOTES

1 Dorothy Gabe Coleman, *Montaigne's 'Essais'* (London, 1987), pp. 18-19.

2 R. A. Sayce, *The Essays of Montaigne: A Critical Exploration* (London, 1972), pp. 303-4.

3 Quoted by Pierre Bonnet, 'Jeux phoniques et jeux de mots dans les *Essais* de Montaigne', *BSAM*, 3e série, XVI (1960), 3-29, p. 3.

4 Thomas Wilson, *Arte of Rhetorique (1553)*, edited by Thomas J. Derrick, (New York, 1982), p. 279.

5 See Antoine Compagnon, 'Montaigne ou la parole donnée', in *Rhétorique de Montaigne: actes du colloque de la Société des Amis de Montaigne (Paris, 14 et 15 décembre 1984)*, edited by Frank Lestringant (Paris, 1985), 9-19.

6 See for example Margaret McGowan, *Montaigne's Deceits: The Art of Persuasion in the 'Essais'* (London, 1974), and *Rhétorique de Montaigne*, op. cit.

7 T. Cave, *The Cornucopian Text: Problems of Writing in the French Renaissance* (Oxford, 1979), p. 141.

8 S. Guazzo, *The Civile Conversation*, introduction by E. Sullivan, (London, 1925), 2 vols, I. 146.

9 See André Berthiaume, 'Montaigne humoriste', *Etudes littéraires* (Uni-0versité Laval), IV, 2 (August 1971), 187-207, p. 187.

10 Berthiaume, art. cit., p. 191.

11 Michel de Montaigne, *The Essayes; or, Moral, Politike and Militarie Discourses of Lo: Michaell de Montaigne* (London, 1969), p. 565.

12 Zoé Samaras, 'La Figure étymologique dans les *Essais* de Montaigne', *BSAM*, 5e série, XIV-XV (1975), 75-80, p. 80. For an abundant list of examples of word-play in the *Essais* see also, by the same author, *The Comic Element of Montaigne's Style* (Paris, 1970).

13 Léopold Peeters, *La Roulette aux mots* (Paris, 1975), p. 10. See also Walter Redfern, *Puns* (Oxford, 1984).

14 'De Montaigne à Boccace et de Boccace à Montaigne: contribution à l'étude de la naissance de l'Essai', in *La Nouvelle française à la Renaissance*, études réunies par Lionello Sozzi (Geneva & Paris, 1981), 13-40.

15 Cf. Noël du Fail, *Contes...d'Eutrapel*, 1585.

16 Quoted in *Les Bigarrures du Seigneur des Accords*, Notes et variantes par Francis Goyet, TLF, 340 (Geneva, 1986), 2 vols, I. XXXIV.

17 See R. A. Sayce and David Maskell, *A Descriptive Bibliography of Montaigne's 'Essais', 1580-1700* (London, 1983), pp. 9-11.
18 See *Les Bigarrures,* ed. cit., I. XIX.
19 Barbara C. Bowen, *Words and the Man in French Renaissance Literature*, French Forum Monographs, 45 (Lexington, 1983), p. 88.
20 Rabelais, *Gargantua*, Prologue, in *Œuvres de François Rabelais*, edited by Abel Lefranc, 5 vols (Paris, 1912-31), I. 7.
21 Berthiaume, art. cit., p. 204.

8

Montaigne's Text:
'Neglegentia Diligens'

Dorothy Gabe Coleman

Montaigne's method of reading is that of a creative writer. He starts not so much with knowledge or scholarship or history but a remark or a chance event or even a quotation that sets his mind rolling. As Henry James once said: 'Experience is never limited, and it is never complete; it is an immense sensibility, a kind of huge spider-web of the finest silken threads suspended in the chamber of consciousness'; and this is true of Montaigne. Reading his own *Essais* makes him at once highly creative but also hyper-critical and sensitive to tiny points, be they stylistic or marks of judgement or experience.

He published the first two books of the *Essais* in Bordeaux in 1580. In September of that year he made a long tour across the Alps to Italy, coming home (after he had been elected to the mayoralty of Bordeaux) on 30 November 1581. In 1582 the second edition of the *Essais* is published with additions (e.g. quotations from Dante and Tasso). We are witnessing a fundamental characteristic of Montaigne's writing: the changes are not merely superficial, as we shall see later. In Paris in 1588, Abel L'Angelier brought out the first two books plus a further book of *Essais*: six hundred additions to the first two, and thirteen chapters of Book III. Between 1588 and his death in September 1592, Montaigne experiences a tremendous creative urge: on the margins of his copy he writes in additions, crosses words out, puts words in, goes back again and again to some of his reflections. This unique copy is now to be found in the Bibliothèque Municipale of Bordeaux and is known as the *exemplaire de Bordeaux*. I shall take a few examples to support my argument from the facsimile of the *exemplaire de Bordeaux* (which is partly in Montaigne's handwriting and partly the published 1588 edition) and the rest from the Villey-Saulnier edition.[1]

Wordsworth said that the poet's aim was to arouse a 'co-operative power in the mind of the reader', and we are aware that Montaigne's words are full of far-off suggestion, that he is trained in rhetoric, which presupposes more than it says, and that our reading of his *Essais* is a conscious effort at entering their 'willful disorder'. We know that the *Essais* are littered with quotations from ancient authors: they are there to thicken the strata of meaning, to ask the reader to consider two contexts instead of one. Montaigne assumes that his reader is neither naïve nor stupid; he assumes also that the reader will have no difficulty in checking the second context — even though he does not even name the writer. How much more obscure is his 'playing' with a text which he never once mentions. Erasmus is a figure used in this way. Hugo Friedrich in his *Montaigne* (published in German in 1949) noted in a footnote that Montaigne's famous definition of style (in 'De l'institution des enfans', I. 26) followed systematically the Erasmian definition as formulated in a letter of 1527. Margaret Mann Phillips demonstrated later that Montaigne's definition of style must be quoting Erasmus but never does he say so.[2] It becomes in Montaigne the defence of the non-professional, the writer who is free and is against the narrowness of the specialist. Recently Gérard Defaux has said that, although they may both have come across something in an ancient author, it is clear that 'Montaigne, le plus souvent, copie directement Erasme sans le dire'.[3] This is one obvious feature of the 'willful disorder' that could be further examined; indeed, in my opinion, more study of the relationship between Erasmus and Montaigne would illuminate the whole problem of 'imitation', or the problem of writing in the Renaissance.[4]

No two generations ever view a literary figure in quite the same way. No two individuals can regard Montaigne in a similar fashion. For example Peter Burke, in his excellent little book, says that 'Montaigne is, in a sense, our contemporary. Few writers of the sixteenth century are easier to read today'.[5] I disagree violently with this view. Montaigne sees in his writing the density, discontinuity, opacity, and obliqueness which disorientate every reader of the *Essais*. As an intelligent critic and creator, Montaigne sends you back to his text and makes you read a passage scrupulously a thousand times. I would say of Montaigne what he said of his dear Plutarch: 'je ne le puis si peu racointer que je n'en tire cuisse ou aile' (III. 5. 875c). Florio puts it rather nicely: 'If I cast but a glance upon him, I pull some legge or wing from him.' Burke's statement that 'Montaigne made no claim to be a literary artist; quite the reverse' (op. cit., p. 58) shows that he is reading him on one level only, and he makes no reference to Montaigne's hand-written notes in the *exemplaire de Bordeaux*. My hypothesis is very different: between 1588 and 1592 Montaigne was consciously artistic. I take EP Pl. 906 and look at the note on the right-hand margin. It is really a tremendous statement:

> C'est l'indiligent lecteur qui pert mon subiect, non pas moi: il s'en trouvera tousiours en un coing quelque mot ~~bien serré: il~~ qui ne laisse pas d'estre...[roughly four different adjectives indecipherable by me] ...bastant quoi qu'il ~~ne~~ soit ~~estendu~~ serré.

In this note the 'indiligent lecteur' gets an ironic, gentle reprimand; Montaigne has already established a role for the reader of his *Essais*: a participating role. Now he can see that his artistry will never be caught by an unconscientious reader. The 'suffisant lecteur' will react to sense impressions, poetic and aesthetic, he will learn to 'nose' the scent and colour of language, he will feel the texture of puns, he will hear the sounds, the assonance, the alliteration, and will be aware of the ambiguity of all communication. The patterning, the weaving and inter-weaving of ideas, impressions, and reactions are so acute that we never feel that we are 'grasping' Montaigne. And the alterations in this page prove that the author was immensely aware of style. Other profound features are in the 1588-92 marginalia. For instance, after the phrase 'I'ayme l'alleure poetique, à sauts et à gambades', there is a little omission mark, and on top of the phrase comes: 'C'est un'art come dict Platon legiere uolage...[two or three words crossed out and inde-cipherable]...demoniacle', which suggests that Plato's method of com-position — at once poetic, flowing easily with a large number of images — is approved of by Montaigne (as his large-scale ideas are disapproved of by him). And sure enough, a few lines down, in a left-hand margin, after the textual phrase: 'Mais la meilleure prose ancienne', comes the comment: 'et ie la seme ceans indifferamment pour uers...'. The prose that Montaigne is composing is a poetic prose. Fantasy, imagination, impulsive drives, inspirations — these are all elements he caresses. And maybe, as I have suggested in an article published in 1986, the exciting critic Longinus, more imaginative than Aristotle, is at the back of Montaigne's mind. I take one last statement from the same marginalia: 'C'est l'originel langage des Dieus.' We can regard it as a confession on the part of Montaigne that he is aware of an inspiration which moves him as if he were rushed by a divine fire or demon.

This 'willful disorder' or what Petronius had called 'curiosa felicitas' (*Satyricon* 118. 5) in evaluating Horace — an author whom Montaigne revered throughout his writing career — can be shown in the variants to the 1588 text. No-one in any literature has given the impression of disorder, of fantasy, and of apparent negligence more than has Montaigne in creating a conscious work of art. His discursiveness is almost always deceptive. A major point in comparing these editions — those of 1580, 1582, and 1587, and L'Angelier's of 1588 — is that they include more and more quotations, are on the whole larger in size and are bolder as the years go by. For example in I. 26, among the teachers he had in the collège de Guyenne he omits Muret in the 1580 edition, but in the 1582 and 1587 editions we find the name of Marc-Antoine Muret added after that of Buchanan. We may remember the discussion he has in Rome with his old teacher as related in the *Journal de voyage*; there is then a plausible reason for adding his name in the new edition of 1582. When Montaigne re-reads his *Essais* we can imagine him noticing that in one sentence of one chapter he is more or less saying something he has already said elsewhere (e.g. Villey-Saulnier, 757). We recall his intense dislike of repeating himself and we can visualise him, pen in hand, crossing out in several swift strokes the sentence in the text.

Another example is singularly interesting from the viewpoint of carelessly stating a precise attitude, and it comes in the fascinating chapter 'De la tristesse' (I. 2). Montaigne discusses extreme 'volupté' which is inseparable from pain; he quotes the famous Catullan poem, itself a 'translation' of Sappho's ode (which had been discovered via Longinus' treatise *On the Sublime*, first published in 1554) and follows it with a personal comment:

Et de là s'engendre par fois la défaillance fortuite, qui surprent les
amoureux si hors de saison, et cette glace qui les saisit par la force
d'une ardeur extreme, au giron mesme de la joüyssance.

(I. 2. 13a)

The poems by Sappho and Catullus are used as examples of vehement
and violent passions: the obsession of lovers with looking at those
they love; the physiological nature of sensations connected with lust;
the speechlessness; the inability to focus except on the loved one; the
tingling of the ears — a sure sign of love; the alternation between fire
and ice and the sheer immobility that love creates. All this is suggested
in Montaigne's quotation and his personal comment. It was in the 1580
edition (see Sayce's bibliography[6]), in the 1582, the 1587 (Iean Richer,
ruë sainct Iean de Latran, à l'Arbre verdoyant, M.D.LXXXVII) and the
Villey-Saulnier edition. But in the 1588 edition, the *exemplaire de
Bordeaux*, he adds after 'joüyssance' the phrase: 'accident qui ne m'est
pas incogneu', a phrase that he swiftly erases. Why does he enter it and
why (maybe years later — at least any time between 1588 and his death
in 1592) does he erase it definitively? Is this a part of his *diligens*
front? Is he ashamed at such a confession of impotence on his part?
The problem of sincerity and insincerity? Maybe.

As a last example of Montaigne re-reading himself and deciding which
focus to give readers of his text I shall take words which are funny,
ambiguous, and again tricky as to his sincerity. They occur in 'De
l'experience' (III. 13), the last and most perfect of his *Essais*:

La decence mesme de ma contenance en compagnie ordinaire n'en est
pas troublée [by his ill health], et porte mon eau sept heures et aussi
longtemps qu'un autre.

(EP Pl. 995)

Seven hours is a fine retention of urine in human beings. Montaigne
re-reads it and sees how he can make it much more impressive; so he
crosses out the 'sept' and puts 'dix' instead! As Emerson said: 'Cut
these words, and they would bleed; they are vascular and alive.'

The examples so far suggest the painstaking way Montaigne has of
correcting his *Essais* and, what is more of a problem, his 'in-joking'

with himself. The wit, irony, modest self-declarations, and pointed remarks in Montaigne are difficult: reading and re-reading him, we perceive eventually the gradations between a serious remark and an ironical one. It is important to know what tone of voice Montaigne is using: his interpreters have gone astray in taking everything he says seriously. For example, critics have taken the first part of the *Apologie* (the comparison between animals and men) on one level only: it is evident that Montaigne, in heaping paradox upon paradox to prove the vileness of man, is more or less amusing himself, just as he is in the chapter 'Des cannibales' (I. 31), when he praises the civilisation of the natives of Brazil as superior to that of his own countrymen. Montaigne sees that the *condition humaine* is at once sensitive and ridiculous. When he is discussing the problem of knowledge, seen in a relativist way, he uses the famous analogy:

> Quand je me jouë à ma chatte, qui sçait si elle passe son temps de moy plus que je ne fay d'elle.
>
> (II. 12. 452c)

Judging Montaigne's claim to practise *neglegentia diligens* is made even more difficult by the text that we have to work with: the Strowski decipherment (the *Edition municipale*, Bordeaux, 1906-33), has been followed by all subsequent editors like Villey, Rat, Plattard, Sacy, Michel and so on. I shall take some examples from the chapter 'De l'exercitation' (II. 6) to show what problems it raises. Just before his quotation from Lucan, Montaigne sums up the attitude of Pompey at his murder: 'They will love me if they admire me in defeat rather than showing grief at my death.' This is followed by an exclamation mark. When we look at the *exemplaire de Bordeaux* (EP Pl. 152), there is no exclamation mark. This is a trifle. Montaigne adds for the 1588 edition the words of Lucan:

> Jus hoc animi morientis habebat.
>
> (He exercised this authority over his soul as he died.)

The true line from Lucan runs: 'mentis erat, ius hoc animi morientis habebat' (VIII. 636). Strowski rather pompously decked the 'ius' with a capital as if it were the beginning of the line, thereby showing his poor understanding of Latin prosody. Montaigne chose, deliberately, to omit the 'mentis erat' since it was the remainder of the line that was relevant to his purpose.[7] Another 1588 passage will show even more clearly Strowski's defects. The passage added begins in this way:

> Je n'imagine aucun estat pour moy si insupportable et horrible, que d'avoir l'ame vifve et affligée, sans moyen de se declarer.
>
> (375b)

Montaigne evokes one of the most horrifying states of physical disorder that any man can expect: to be struck with aphasia, caused by the destruction of a special region of the brain, the cortex, which in right-handed people is set near the left cerebral hemisphere. The patient sees words and letters perfectly but they seem like unintelligible cyphers to him. This lesion of the brain means, sometimes, the total inability to get out sounds which are intelligible in plain simple terms. Re-reading the sentence after 1588 Montaigne with, it seems to me, a shudder, puts in an exclamation mark. (This is visible in the *exemplaire de Bordeaux* in facsimile, but it is even clearer in Montaigne's own copy in the Bibliothèque Municipale of Bordeaux.) Everyone knows the manner of Montaigne's death: he was struck, three days before his death on 13 September 1592, with a paralysis of the tongue; he could only communicate with his fellows by means of writing. It is as if he had foreseen this state in the 1588 edition and he shows his emotional horror via his exclamation mark. This, of course, was not seen by Strowski.

The importance of death is a leitmotiv of the *Essais*. Yet a statement by Bowman that 'he remained conscious and intelligent through his three days of agony to the very end' is misleading, for we have only second-hand accounts of his approach to death.[8] Again, Burke says: 'He had achieved that serenity which he once defined as the distinguishing mark of wisdom' (op. cit., p. 66); that is broadly true, but we think of 'Sur des vers de Virgile' (III. 5), where illness and old age are part of the texture in 1588-92: illness 'affesse mon esprit, le clouë et faict un effect contraire' (844c); and a little marginal comment like 'et le mauvais estat de nostre santé'. The years after 1588 are not bright: his health is deteriorating fast; he has fewer chances for scintillating conversation; solitude is his fate:

> Decrepitude is a solitary quality. I am sociable even unto excesse, yet doe I thinke it reasonable at last to substract my opportunity from the sight of the world, and hatch it in myself. Let me shrowd and shrugge myselfe into my shell as a tortoise, and learne to see men without taking hold of them. I should outrage them in so steepe a passage. It is now high time to turne from the compagny.
>
> (Florio, p. 502)

This is Montaigne at his most mature, accepting the facts of ageing and dying and accepting too the unsociableness of old age, decayed and enfeebled with infirmities: 'So do our minutes hasten to their end.' And yet, his imagination, his wit and humour vibrate and he makes a simile — comparing his retreat to that of a tortoise in its shell — which is entrancingly witty and most humane.

Entrancing and most humane is the pronouncement he makes about himself on the subject of his old age.[9] There are five adverbs that he plays with here. First: 'Or la vieillesse a un peu besoin d'estre traictée plus doucement et plus delicatement.' Secondly, he crosses these out in favour of 'bassement...facilement'; but they do not convey his feeling about old age and they seem inferior to the first two. He erases them and in the space between them writes *the* adverb, 'tendrement'; this adverb is the most sensitive of the five. The flavour of delicate tenderness is caught here and communicated subtly to the reader; it is part of Montaigne's sensibility which makes personal emotion of immense value in the study of other men. Here we can 'feel' that the gap between 'je suis moy-mesmes la matiere de mon livre' (I. 'Au lecteur', 3a) and 'chaque homme porte la forme entiere de l'humaine condition' (III. 2. 805b) has closed. Montaigne wants men to stretch gently, delicately, and kindly to other men in their closing years; sympathy and tenderness are desired in love and friendship. In this 'vivre coliqueux' (II. 37. 759a) 'Je ne vise pas de ce costé là, je m'ayme trop' (III. 7. 916b) he fears, and yet 'Quand je pourroy me faire craindre, j'aimeroy encore mieux me faire aymer' (II. 8. 393a).

110

All these examples could be concluded upon: the omission of Erasmus is conscious negligence; the examples from 'De la tristesse' can be treated seriously; the 'sincerity' of Montaigne is ambiguous; the Strowski examples point to the defects of the text which is the only one available at this stage; the last example is of the painstaking way Montaigne seeks out the unique quality of life/death/old age/affection for the whole of mankind. But they seem to me to point to a third Montaigne (which, as usual, he saw first): not the 'real, living Montaigne', nor the writer of the *Essais*, but:

Je n'ay pas plus faict mon livre que mon livre m'a faict, livre consubstantiel à son autheur, d'une occupation propre, membre de ma vie.

(II. 18. 665c)

Indeed, it is another person that we get to know in the *Essais*:

il m'a fallu si souvent dresser et composer pour m'extraire, que le patron s'en est fermy et aucunement formé soy-mesmes. Me peignant pour autry [*sic*], je me suis peint en moy de couleurs plus nettes que n'estoyent les miennes premieres.

(*ibidem*)

Montaigne knows full well that he becomes someone who is not what he is. He reads Montaigne in the same way that he reads Plutarch. He takes up a point, re-writes it in the variants of all the texts of the *Essais* — from 1572(?) until 1592 — knowing that it seems a 'betrayal' of what he had once thought, but it was a *trahison* 'de bonne foi'. He demands of a reader the full awareness of what he is trying to do:

Poetry often creates an idiosyncratic and symbolic world, a world in which all the senses cooperate, in which thought and feeling are conjoined, and the physical is scarcely distinguishable from the moral. Poetry is capable of creating a pattern neither chronological nor linear, a pattern which demands of the reader not a cumulative process of semantic addition, but a holding in suspension of many particles which multiply together rather than adding up to a prescribed sum...It is perhaps in the rendering of what is most essentially human, what is almost unnameable and unsayable — the sensation of being, at its most inward, most particular, and paradoxically most universal — that poetry excels.[10]

NOTES

1 *Reproduction en phototypie de l'exemplaire avec notes manuscrites marginales des Essais de Montaigne appartenant à la ville de Bordeaux*, edited by Fortunat Strowski, 3 vols (Paris, 1912). Abbreviated to EP.

2 'From the *Ciceronianus* to Montaigne', in *Classical Influences in European Culture, A.D. 1500-1700*, edited by R. R. Bolgar (Cambridge, 1976), 191-7.

3 *Marot, Rabelais, Montaigne: l'écriture comme présence* (Paris & Geneva, 1987), p. 42.

4 For a pioneering analysis of this problem see Terence Cave, *The Cornucopian Text: Problems of Writing in the French Renaissance* (Oxford, 1979).

5 *Montaigne* (Oxford, 1981), p. 1.

6 R. A. Sayce, *The Essays of Montaigne: A Critical Exploration* (London, 1972).

7 *Les Essais de Michel de Montaigne*, edited by Strowski, Gebelin, and Villey (Edition Municipale), 5 vols (Bordeaux, 1906-33). Abbreviated to EM.
The worst kind of 'modernisation' that the EM has is that of altering the colon into a semi-colon. It is quite clear that when we read either the original or the EP we can see semi-colons used by Montaigne. Look at one page of the EP Pl. 764:

    EP has a comma after *an*. EM omits it.
    EP has a colon after *eniouée*. EM has a comma.
    EP has a comma after *stupide*. EM omits it.
    EP has a comma after *compaignie*. EM omits it.
    EP has a comma after *France*. EM omits it.
    EP has a comma after *resseante*. EM omits it.
    EP has a semi-colon after *paume*. EM has a comma.
    EP has a comma after *essays*. EM omits it.
    EP has a comma after *esprit*. EM omits it.

EP wants to make short, simple, attacking sentences. Thus we find a capital on Q and on L. EM ignores this.

EP has a comma after *corps*. EM omits it.

EP has a comma after *coups*. EM omits it.

EP has a colon after *royales*. EM has a comma.

EP has a full stop after *colligeance*. EM has a comma.

EP has a comma after *propres*. EM omits it.

EP has the top dot of a colon crossed to become a comma. EM has a colon.

EP has a comma before a quotation. EM has a colon.

And, throughout, the EM punctuates the marginalia. (EM vol. III. 73)

8 *Montaigne: Essays* (London, 1965), p. 35.

9 EP Pl. 1019.

10 Valerie Minogue, *Nathalie Sarraute and the War of the Words: A Study of Five Novels* (Edinburgh, 1981), p. 29.

List of Texts Cited

The book and chapter number, and the title of the chapter, are followed by page references to the present volume.

List of Texts Cited

Index

(Mythological and fictional names are given in italics. All other names are written in Roman script. Modern literary critics are included where they are cited in the main text of the papers.)

Index